CELEBRATION
THE · BOOK · OF
JEWISH FESTIVALS

Consulting Editor   Naomi Black

Rosh Hashana and Yom Kippur	Yossi Prager
Sukkot	Yehuda Najman
Chanukah	Jeffrey Kuperman
Purim	Daniel Feit
Passover	Elihu Siegman
Shavuot	Eli Clark
Anthologists	Solomon Schneider Larry Kwass
Song Adaptations	Debbie Gilmore
Recipes	Naomi Black
Crafts	Linda Hebert

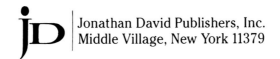

Jonathan David Publishers, Inc.
Middle Village, New York 11379

Published in the United States by
Jonathan David Publishers, Inc.,
68-22 Eliot Avenue, Middle Village,
New York 11379.

Library of Congress Cataloging-in-Publication Data

Celebration—the book of Jewish festivals.
  Includes index.
    1. Fasts and feasts—Judaism. I. Black, Naomi,
  1957–
  BM690.C44   1987   296.4′ 3   86–24292

ISBN: 0-8246-0340-0

Consulting Editor: Naomi Black
Art Director: Rod Gonzalez
Designed by S and M Graphics
Photo Editor: Barbara Glasgow
Principal Photographer: Keith Glasgow
Production Manager: Karen L. Greenberg
Food Preparation and Display: Marcy Ringel

Typeset by BPE Graphics, Inc.
Color separations by South Seas Graphic Art Company
Printed and bound in China by Leefung-Asco Printers Ltd.

This book was prepared and produced by
Tern Enterprises Inc.

ACKNOWLEDGMENTS

Grateful acknowledgment is due the following publishers and organizations for the use of the material mentioned below.

Jewish Frontier magazine: "The Sound of Seders," by Ree Goodman (April 1978); *A Yom Kippur Tale* by Rabbi Samuel H. Dresner (September 1966).

Jewish Spectator magazine: "Rosh Hashanah," by Joyce B. Schwartz (Fall 1978); "Seder 5732," by Robert Cowan (March 1972).

Reconstructionist magazine: "Hallel," by Carol Adler (November 1981).

Schocken Publishing House Ltd. of Tel Aviv, Israel: "The Celebrants," from *The Bridal Canopy*, by S. Y. Agnon, copyright 1937.

Union of American Hebrew Congregations: "For Hanukkah," by Hayyim Nahman Bialik, translated by Jessie E. Sampter from *Far Over the Sea: Poems and Jingles for Children*, copyright 1939.

Union of Sephardic Congregations: "The Banquet of Esther," by Yehudah Halevi, translated by David de Sola Pool.

A special note of thanks goes to Sharon Squibb, without whose unrelenting help this book could not have been published.

Thanks are also due to Rhona Bitner, who so generously donated her time and photographic skills to the book by allowing us to use her many scenic shots of Israel; to Yaacov Luria, winner of a Saxton Fellowship from Harper and Row, and who is at work on a memoir and a collection of his published work, many of which appeared in *World Over,* a magazine for children formerly published by the Jewish Education Committee; to Nancy Golden and Shoshannah Walker for their permission to use transparencies of their beautifully crafted works; to S and M Graphics, who designed the book so well; to Jamie Harrison for the permission to use her recipe for Drunken Pound Cake; to Andrea Soorikian for her crafts idea and instructions for the Wheat Basket Centerpiece; to Marcy Ringel for food preparation and display; and to Michael Riesenberg, Louise Quayle, Karla Olson, and lastly, to John Bralower.

CONTENTS

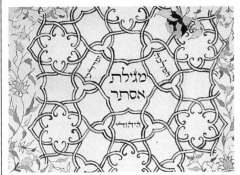

INTRODUCTION

Imaginative, practical, and beautifully il-lustrated, *CELEBRATION: The Book of Jewish Festivals* is designed to help you and your family understand and enjoy the major Jewish holidays: Rosh Hashana and Yom Kippur, Sukkot, Chanukah, Purim, Passover, and Shavuot.

Each chapter offers an interpretation of the traditions, balancing explanations of the basic rituals with more sophisti-cated ways of looking at the festivals. You'll learn that according to the Midrash, Purim is the only holiday that will continue in the world to come, how Passover is also called the "night of anticipation," and why there is a special emphasis on women to light the Chanukah candles.

Poems, songs, and read-aloud stories, some old and some new, provide entertainment as well as history for the children. The Story of Ruth, of Esther, and of the Maccabees are all here, along with the lesser-known stories of Rav Amnon, Reb Yozifel, and Judith.

You'll also find mouth-watering menus for each holiday, complete with delicious, up-to-date recipes for dishes from Apple Cake to Tzimmes. The traditional blends with the innovative: the Seder menu high-lights two kinds of Charoses and Citrus Sponge Cake *and* a more modern Endive, Watercress, and Beet Salad. For Shavuot, cooks will take delight in the recipes for Poached Snapper with Ravigote Sauce and Berry Charlotte, as well as the more traditional Blintzes and Kugel.

Each chapter also includes amusing or elegant crafts ideas, many of which are simple enough for youngsters to make. Created especially for *CELEBRATION*, the crafts focus on brightening the holidays: New Year's cards, a dreidl and Chanukah wall hanging; king and queen costumes for Purim, and more, including step-by-step instructions for making an elegant matzo cover and tissue flowers for Shavuot.

Brimming with just the right combination of respect and joy, *CELE-BRATION* encourages observance and rejoicing—and brings the holi-days into your home for the whole family to enjoy.

ROSH HASHANA

The New Year

Thirty days before Rosh Hashana, on the first day of the month of Elul, many Sephardic Jews rise before dawn every morning to recite the *selichot,* prayers of repentance. Ashkenazic Jews begin saying selichot a week before Rosh Hashana. For all Jews, the period encompassing Elul and the first ten days of Tishrei is a distinctive time—when God feels especially close to His people. Following the general principle of "Seek God when He is to be found; call to Him when He is near (Isaiah Jews seize this period to ask forgiveness for their sins and pray for a prosperous year.

Why did God choose these days in particular? For this, one must return thousands of years, back to the first Shavuot in the history of the Jewish people. On the sixth day of Sivan, God gave His nation a special gift—His holy Torah. On that day, Moses joyously ascended Mount Sinai to receive and study the Torah. Forty days later, he descended, only to find the Jews worshiping the Golden Calf. In his ire—and with God's approval—Moses broke the tablets of the Torah, symbolically severing God's covenant with the Jews. Moses again traveled up the mountain, this time to plead for the Jewish people. When Moses returned, God commanded him to ascend the mountain once more. On the first day of the seventh month—Elul—Moses climbed Mount Sinai one last time. Forty days later, on the tenth day of Tishrei, he brought down with him the tangible sign of God's forgiveness and love, the Second Tablets. This love is reflected even in the Hebrew spelling of *Elul,* an acronym for *Ani L'dodi V'dodi Li* ("I am for my beloved and my beloved is for me"), a verse from the *Song of Songs* that

emphasizes the close bond between God and His chosen people.

The Torah sets aside the first day of Tishrei (Rosh Hashana) as a "memorial proclaimed with the blast of the *shofar,* a holy day." The tenth day (Yom Kippur) is set aside for atonement: "For on this day, He will forgive you to purify you from all your sins; before God you will be pure." Repentance, however, is not an event; it is a process through which a person recognizes the distance that has come between himself and God, resolves to close the gap, and commits himself to returning to Torah and its commandments. The forty days between the first of Elul and Yom Kippur offer man time to reflect, to resolve, and to act, culminating with a reenactment of history—a renewed acceptance of the holy Torah.

Traditions: Rosh Hashana

Today is the birthday of the world; today God will sit in judgment over all the world's creations (from the Rosh Hashana *mussaf* service).

Rosh Hashana is a day on which each person individually, and the nations of the world collectively, are judged by an omniscient, omnipotent God. Such a day would seem to call for sadness rather than rejoicing, fasts rather than feasts.

Torahs, right, respectfully covered in silk, velvet, or other fine cloth and ornamented with decorative crowns, are considered the most holy documents in Judaism.

Many holiday menus include sweets, carrots, apples, honey and nuts.

Go, eat choice foods and drink sweet drinks, for the day is holy to our God. Do not be sad, for your rejoicing in God is the source of your strength. (Nehemiah 8:10)

And yet, Jewish law forbids fasting on Rosh Hashana. Why?

And if Rosh Hashana is the day on which God meticulously reviews one's every action, the Rosh Hashana prayer service should contain a section for confession—recited ten times on Yom Kippur but *not* on Rosh Hashana. Why?

The answer lies in the opening to Rav Amnon's (see "The Story of Rav Amnon," page 19) incisive prayer:

Let us give strength to this holy day, for it is solemn and awe-inspiring. On it Your dominion will be exalted, Your throne will be established in mercy, and You will occupy it in truth.

On Rosh Hashana Jews commemorate God's creation of the world. He alone created; He alone commands the earth below and the sky above. Rosh Hashana is the annual coronation of the King of Kings, a ceremony glorified by the Jewish people's observance of it. Both the liturgy and the festive meal demonstrate and celebrate our acceptance of God as the ultimate ruler.

This absolute sovereign, however, is also the supreme judge. Rosh Hashana combines two related themes: It celebrates the dominion of the King of Kings, the mighty God of the Jewish people, while it instills the awe and fear that people must feel before the king pronounces judgment over his subjects.

The Talmud quotes: "Say before me *malchiot, zichroniot,* and *shofarot:* Malchiot so that you place my reign over you, zichroniot so that I remember you [for health and happiness on this day of judgment], and how should you do this? With a shofar."

The first imperative on Rosh Hashana is to proclaim God's eternal dominion. Malchiot, a string of biblical verses discussing divine sovereignty, serve this purpose. The zichroniot verses raise memories of past salvations by God, the omniscient judge who will pass sentence on this awe-inspiring day. To elicit both divine dominion and mercy, the ram's horn—the shofar—is sounded.

The blowing of the shofar is the only specific commandment for Rosh Hashana. The shofar is recognized as *the* Rosh Hashana symbol by all ages of people, and a most fitting symbol it is, for its one hundred blasts nobly suggest and reinforce the day's dual theme. Just as trumpeters announce the presence of a mortal king, Jews proclaim the coronation of the King of Kings. Yet, the shofar also promotes introspection; each loud, simple

Jews from throughout the world travel to the Western Wall in Jerusalem, above. At right, *a mosaic tells the story of Abraham and Isaac.*

blast reminds one of imminent divine judgment. The ram's horn is an especially appropriate symbol, for it reminds the Jewish people as well as the Almighty of Abraham's willingness to sacrifice his son, Isaac, to fulfill God's command. At the very last second, God ordered Abraham to replace Isaac with a sacrificial ram. The Torah reading for the second day of Rosh Hashana is "The Sacrifice of Isaac" (Genesis 22), again recalling the patriarch's absolute devotion.

The traditions associated with the holiday are simple and symbolic. After services, people leave the synagogue, saying to each other: "May you be inscribed in the Book of Life." Families then gather for the holiday meal, festive but serious, in keeping with the nature of the day. Usually on the first night of Rosh Hashana, the meal begins with apple dipped in honey to represent a sweet year. After the afternoon meal on the first day of Rosh Hashana, the community might congregate by a riverside, to symbolically throw its sins into the river.

One explanation for this tradition is derived from a *midrash* that describes Abraham's trip to sacrifice Isaac on Mount Moriah. Satan created a river along the path to prevent Abraham from fulfilling God's wish. Abraham entered the water and continued in until it reached his neck. Then, he looked upward and said, "Almighty God, Isaac and I are traveling to sanctify Your name; if we

drown, who will spread your word throughout the nations?"

As Rav Amnon lay in synagogue, dying, he completed the prayer we know today as "U'netane Tokef." His eloquent words bear the Rosh Hashana spirit in their poetry, their intensity, and their awe:

> And a great shofar is blown, and a silent whisper is heard. And the angels quake, and fear seizes them.... And all earthly beings pass before You like sheep. Just as a shepherd counts his flock, so will You count every living being and assign a judgment for all.
>
> On Rosh Hashana their judgment is written and on Yom Kippur it is sealed: How many will pass on and how many will be born; who will live and who shall die;... who by stoning and who by strangling; who will be at ease and who will wander;... who will be poor and who will be rich; who will be lowered and who will be elevated.
>
> And repentance and prayer and charity cancel the harsh decree.

Traditions: Yom Kippur

A man once came to the Kotzker Rebbe with a problem.

"Rebbe," he said, "My family is poor, two of my children are sick, and I can't find a job. Will you please help me?"

The Kotzker replied, "What do you need me for? Just pray to God and He will help."

"But Rebbe, I don't know how to pray."

"Then indeed, you do have a problem."

The blowing of the shofar is the only specific commandment for Rosh Hashana: "Then you shall transmit a blast on the horn; in the seventh month, on the tenth day of the month, the day of Yom Kippur, you shall have the horn sounded throughout the land...And proclaim liberty throughout all the land unto all the inhabitants thereof." (Leviticus 25)

By Yom Kippur, thirty-nine days of repentance have passed. The completely righteous and absolute sinners have been judged on Rosh Hashana. The rest have been given a ten-day reprieve. As men and women review their misdeeds of the past year some become so emotional that they break down into tears. To the very religious, their future—career, health, family—hangs on the twenty-four hours of Yom Kippur, and so they cry out in prayer.

One tale, of one's struggle with prayer, is particularly appropriate on Yom Kippur.

A young boy, age five or six, was impressed by the Russian army. As he grew older, he retained a simple cognizance of his Jewish heritage, despite Russian urging to forget. Then, in his teens, the spark in his soul suddenly ignited, filling him with the desire to return to Jewish tradition. He found a synagogue, in which men wrapped in prayer shawls cried out to God even into the late afternoon. He remembered: "Today is Yom Kippur." Childhood memories began to return, and, reflecting over his years of separation, the adolescent began to weep. He entered the synagogue and opened

a prayer book. The letters seemed familiar, but he couldn't put them together into words. Turning his eyes toward heaven, he cried, "God, all I remember is the Hebrew alphabet. I will read the letters; You put them into words, into sentences, into paragraphs. And forgive me." And God did.

Words alone do not constitute prayer. The true Yom Kippur sacrifice is a humbled heart striving to reach upward to heaven. Yom Kippur is not a day for doing; there is no shofar to blow, no meal to eat, no communal gathering at the riverside. Only prohibitions: Jews may not eat or drink; they may not wash or anoint themselves; they cannot wear leather shoes; and they must refrain from sexual relations.

Yet the day is not a sad one. On all other fasts, the Jewish people mourn various stages in the tragic destruction of the Temple. On Yom Kippur, a final opportunity for redemption has been granted. And although the entire world is judged on this day, the Jewish people as a community have been promised a redemption. To fast on Yom Kippur is not to mourn but to share in the holy day by emulating the heavenly angels who neither eat nor drink, wash nor anoint. Jews, too, allow nothing to distract their thoughts—personal and communal—from spiritual service of the Almighty God.

The yad, at left, is used as a pointer to keep hands from soiling the Torah. A soiled Torah is unusable. Young boys are blessed on Rosh Hashana, below. The plate, right, reads: Rosh Hashana.

People are human, however, and the Talmud acknowledges this: "He who eats on the ninth of Tishrei [and fasts on the tenth], it is as if he had fasted both the ninth and the tenth." Yom Kippur is a fast day, but the day before Yom Kippur is devoted to eating. Even learning the Torah is minimized so that one may eat more than usual. The Torah recognizes that eating gives strength for the fast day to follow. Some scholars have suggested a deeper meaning for this unusual custom. Prayer is spiritual; eating is basic, instinctive. Judaism challenges man to elevate eating to the spiritual realm by considering it nourishment to enhance the service of God. On the day before Yom Kippur, we realize this ideal, by transforming ingestion and digestion into a preparation for the holy day.

On the eve of Yom Kippur, the entire community—men, women, and children—congregates in the synagogue. The men put on prayer shawls (not normally worn at night) and *kittels,* snow-white robes reflecting the purity of the day. Traditionally, people use the last few minutes before evening to make peace with neighbors and friends, because sins between one person and another person need the forgiveness of the injured party before God will grant a pardon. Only repentance can erase sins between the individual and God. Then, as night falls, the cantor begins the "Kol Nidre." The "Kol Nidre" signifies the absolution of past vows unkept and the desire to avoid future ones. Its importance lies in the great emphasis the Torah places on keeping vows; violating an oath is one of the worst sins. The cantor chants the "Kol Nidre" three times, each time in a

louder voice, allowing its touching melody to evoke the day's holy spirit.

Ma'ariv introduces an integral part of each Yom Kippur service—the *vidui*, confession. Arranged alphabetically, the sets of confessions serve both to help a person reflect over the breadth of his misdeeds and to confess them verbally as part of the formal repentance procedure. One must recite as part of his confession, "Before I was created I was of no worth, and now that I have been created, it is as if I had not been created" with sincerity.

The confessions are all said in the plural (*We* are guilty...). In fact, because the sense of community and unity is such an integral part of Jewish life most of Jewish prayer is written in plural form, even if that requires changing a biblical verse from the singular. "All of Israel is responsible one for another." Your joy is my joy; your pain is my pain; your sin is my sin; your good deed is my good deed.

The bulk of the mussaf service on Yom Kippur is devoted to a review of the High Priest's Yom Kippur duties in the days of the Temple. Historically, only on this day, the holiest day, could the High Priest enter the Holy of Holies, to plead for his people. Five times the High Priest would purify himself in the ritual bath; five times would he change his priestly clothes. The trip into the Holy of Holies was dangerous: An unworthy High Priest would be struck dead upon entering the room. (A rope was tied tautly around his waist; should it go limp, he would be pulled out.) One of the happiest poems of the service describes the face of the High Priest after he exited the Holy of Holies safely: "like the clearest canopy of heaven, like the grace reflected in the groom's face." The poem continues on a sad, realistic note: Today we have neither Temple nor High Priest.

Of the many Yom Kippur sacrifices, the most unusual is described in Leviticus 16. Two similar goats were set aside, and the High Priest drew lots to decide their destinies. One goat he sacrificed in the Temple; the other—the scapegoat—was led into the wilderness by a special messenger and thrown over a cliff. The scapegoat symbolically represented the people of Israel. Its purpose: to drive the Jewish nation to repent. While the First Temple stood, a red ribbon was tied around the scapegoat's neck; if the Jews had repented, it would miraculously turn snow-white—a divine sign of forgiveness.

Yom Kippur seems to pass too quickly. Jews all over have not completed enumerating their sins, not yet firmly committed themselves anew to Torah values or commandments. Yet only an hour remains. The service called *ne'ila*, closing [of the heavenly gates], offers a final opportunity for repentance. Ne'ila is shorter than the other services; much of the confessions have been left out. Instead of asking God to inscribe for life, we beg Him to seal a pleasant judgment. Time is almost out. The service closes with the recitation—seven times—of the verse, "The Lord is our God." The King has been coronated. He has judged. And promised mercy to his faithful people. The shofar is sounded once, and, in unison, the congregation proclaims, "Next year in Jerusalem." Yom Kippur is over.

282 BOOK OF LIFE			283 BOOK OF LIFE		
IN MEMORY OF		HEBREW CALENDAR / NEW CALENDAR	IN MEMORY OF		NEW CALENDAR
CARRIE	WISE	JAN. 9 - '32	Louis Redman		Jan 20 '54
DORE	HIRSH	19 - '19⁰⁰ JAN. 19 - 1900	Abner Blumberg		Jan 22 '67
LOUIS	KAUFMAN	3 - '52	Ruth Korn		Jan 25 '66
LEON	WASSERMAN	17 - '48	Rose Silver		Jan 2 '68
ESTHER	BLICHER	17 - '57	Benjamin Ammerman		Jan 22 '69
BETTY	KRAMER	14 - 63	Sophie G. Wolfe		Jan 24 '70
THEODORE D. SPRITZER		2 F 65	Benjamin Kitay		Jan 11 '45
MARTIN	KOVATCH	6 - 65	Raphael Taub		Jan 11 '74
SYLVIA G. TAUB		27 45	Barnet Elihu Hoffman		Jan 27 '70
LEO SHEP BOLTER		J 24 66	Abbi Lipman		Jan 14 80
NAPTHALI MELTZER		1 67	Rae Levinston		Jan 19 '31
THEODORE SILVER		Jan 13 38	LEO LABRAN		JAN 4 '78

The Story of Rav Amnon

Adapted by Larry Kwass

This story concerns Rav Amnon of Mainz. He was the greatest of the generation, rich, and of distinguished lineage, besides being quite a handsome man. The noblemen and ruler of the town soon began to ask Rav Amnon to convert to their religion, but he refused to listen to them. Daily they entreated him, and daily he refused. The ruler pressured him quite forcefully.

And it happened one day that they were particularly persistent. Rav Amnon said, "I wish to take counsel and think about this matter until the end of three days." (He said this only to push them away from him.) He had only just left from his visit before the ruler, when he chided himself for having let a shade of doubt leave his mouth. How could he need any time to think of whether he would deny God?

He entered his house and was neither able to eat nor drink. Soon he fell ill. All his relatives and loved ones came to comfort him, but he refused to be consoled. He said, "How will I go down to the grave in mourning?" and wept, for his heart was saddened.

And it came to pass on the third day, as he was pained and worried, that the ruler sent for him. Rav Amnon said, "I will not go." So the enemy sent more officers, a larger and more distinguished group than the first, but still he refused to go with them.

The ruler then said, "Hurry and bring Rav Amnon by force." So they hurried and brought him.

The ruler said to him, "What is this, Amnon? Why didn't you come to me at the time you designated to reply to me and do my bidding?"

Rav Amnon offered his answer: "I will determine my own verdict. The tongue that spoke deceitfully to you should, by right, be cut out. (For Rav Amnon wanted to sanctify the Name for having thus spoken.)

Replied the ruler, "No, I will not cut out the tongue, for you spoke correctly. Rather, the legs which did not come at the appointed time I will cut, and the rest of your body will go free." The ruler commanded his men to cut off the fingers and toes of Rav Amnon's hands and feet. As they severed his limbs, at each joint they would ask him, "Do you want to switch to our faith, Amnon?" and he would answer, "No." As they finished cutting, the ruler commanded that they lay Rav Amnon in a shield with his fingers at his side, and they sent him to his house.

Soon thereafter the time for Rosh Hashana arrived. Rav Amnon requested that his relatives carry him to the synagogue with all his fingers preserved in salt, and seat him by the cantor. They did so, and when the cantor reached the *Kedushah* (sanctification prayer), "And the heavenly creatures...," Rav Amnon told him, "Wait a moment and I will sanctify the Great Name."

He then, in a loud voice, called out "To You sanctification should rise up." [That is to say, "I have sanctified Your Name, Your sovereignty and Unity."] He then said, "Let us declare the power of the holiness of the day" (*Un'taneh tokef k'dushat hayom*). And "It is true that You are the Judge and Rebuker.... The seal of each man's hand is in it [The Book of Judgment] and You remember the souls of all living [for so Rav Amnon was judged on Rosh Hashana]."

When he finished the closing prayer he died and was lost from the world in front of all. "And he is not anymore, for the Lord took him."

Three days after his purification (prior to burial), Rav Amnon appeared in a dream to Rabbi Kalonymos son of Rabbi Meshulam. He taught him the prayer, *"Un'taneh Tokef k'dushat hayom."* Rav Amnon commanded him to spread it among all the areas of the dispersion, that it should be a testimony and a remembrance. And he did so.

Rosh Hashanah

Beneath the iridescent dome
The shofar sounds,
Reverberates,
Shocking the eardrums of memory,
Focusing the mind.
Black-frocked men rock
In timeless rhythm,
Smooth undulations,
A ceaseless paean of faith
Striking melancholy chords
To internal music.

—JOYCE B. SCHWARTZ

The New Year
Rosh-Hashanah, 5643 (1882)

Not while the snow-shroud round dead earth is rolled,
And naked branches point to frozen skies,—
When orchards burn their lamps of fiery gold,
The grape glows like a jewel, and the corn
A sea of beauty and abundance lies,
    Then the new year is born.

Look where the mother of the months uplifts
    In the green clearness of the unsunned West,
Her ivory horn of plenty, dropping gifts,
    Cool, harvest-feeding dews, fine-winnowed light;
Tired labor with fruition, joy and rest
        Profusely to requite.

Blow, Israel, the sacred cornet! Call
    Back to thy courts whatever faint heart throb
With thine ancestral blood, thy need craves all.
    The red, dark year is dead, the year just born
Leads on from anguish wrought by priest and mob,
        To what undreamed-of morn?

For never yet, since on the holy height,
    The Temple's marble walls of white and green
Carved like the sea-waves, fell, and the world's light
    Went out in darkness,—never was the year
Greater with potent and with promise seen,
        Than this eve now and here.

Even as the Prophet promised, so your tent
    Hath been enlarged unto earth's farthest rim.
To snow-capped Sierras from vast steppes ye went,
    Through fire and blood and tempest-tossing wave,
For freedom to proclaim and worship Him,
        Mighty to slay and save.

High above flood and fire ye held the scroll,
    Out of the depths ye published still the Word.
No bodily pang had power to swerve your soul:
    Ye, in a cynic age of crumbling faiths,
Lived to bear witness to the living Lord,
        Or died a thousand deaths.

In two divided streams the exiles part,
    One rolling homeward to its ancient source,
One rushing sunward with fresh will, new heart.
    By each the truth is spread, the law unfurled,
Each separate soul contains the nation's force,
        And both embrace the world.

Kindle the silver candle's seven rays,
    Offer the first fruits of the clustered bowers,
The garnered spoil of bees. With prayer and praise
    Rejoice that once more tried, once more we prove
How strength of supreme suffering still is ours
        For Truth and Law and Love.

—EMMA LAZARUS

Kol Nidre

Kol nid - rë____ ve-e-sa - rë____ v'-ha-ra - më____ v'-ko-na-

më ____ v'-hi - nu - yë____ v'-ki-nu - së____ u -sh'-

v - ot. Din _____ - dar __ -

na u - d'-ish _____ t' - va ____ - na u - d'

a _____ - ha - rim __ - na. V' - di ____ - a -

sar ____ - na __ - al __ - naf - sha - ta ____ - na. ____

A Yom Kippur Tale

by Rabbi Samuel H. Dresner

One Yom Kippur evening Rabbi Levi Yitzhak of Berditchev stood before the Ark to chant the Kol Nidre. It was almost an hour that he stood there, silent, without uttering a word. The sun had already sunk among the the trees. The time for Kol Nidre was almost past, and still he stood there, and did not chant the prayer. Then he bestirred himself, turned to the people and asked the *shamash:*

"Is Berel the tailor here?"

"No, master," replied the shamash.

"Go out," commanded Levi Yitzhak, "and find him."

The shamash went out, found Berel the tailor, and brought him to the synagogue.

"Berel," asked Rabbi Levi Yitzhak, "why do you delay the prayers of Israel?"

"What should I do, my lord," answered Berel. "There is no one before whom I can summon *Him* to judgment. Would our rabbi act as judge in this case?"

"Commence," said Rabbi Levi Yitzhak, "and state your claim."

So Berel began to plead:

"The week before *selichot,* the Count called me to his estate to make a new fur coat for the winter season, which was not too far off. I took my tools and some bread in a sack (for I would not eat the bread made by Gentiles) and went to the manor of the *poritz.* He gave me a number of beautiful skins, soft and rich, out of which I should make the coat.

"I thought to myself: I am a poor man. All my earnings have gone to raise my sons. Now my daughter is reaching the age of marriage and I have not been able to find the means to provide her with a dowry and wedding. Here is a way to fulfill my duty to my daughter. I shall leave ten pelts over, that they may serve as part of a dowry for my daughter. No one will be the wiser....

"And so I did just as I planned. I sewed the coat for the Count with all the skill for which I am known, and still had left over ten pelts for myself. But how would I find a way to take the furs out of the house of the Count? Then a thought occurred to me. When the time for my departure came, I took my loaf of bread, removed the inside, stuffed the pelts within the crust, put the bread in my sack, which I threw over my back, and was on my way.

"I had not gone two miles when I heard a rider behind me on horseback, chasing me. Woe and alas! A terrible fear seized me, for I was certain that the theft had been discovered and I was to be arrested and sent to prison for at least ten years. Quickly I hid my sack under a tree, sat down on the grass, and waited for the rider, my heart throbbing as if to burst.

" 'Berkah, return to the manor!' commanded the rider. 'The Count wants you.'

"I returned to the Count, and believe me, when I entered the room where he sat, the fear of death was upon me. Who knows, I thought, what my punishment would be?

" 'Berkah,' the Count said to me, 'look at this! Is this what you call finishing your work? You forgot to sew a strap on the inside fur by which to hang up my coat.'

"I heaved a sigh of relief and gave thanks to the Almighty. I sewed on the strap, went briskly on my way once again, hastening to the tree where I had hidden the sack that contained the key to my daughter's happiness. But when I came to the tree, lo and behold, my sack was nowhere to be found! No sack, no bread, no pelts. I searched until my arms and legs ached, but nothing helped. They were gone! Then I sat down and began to turn the matter over in my mind, considering it from every angle. At last the truth dawned upon me. This was no other than *His* work." Here Berel pointed up towards Heaven. "*He* does not want a Jew, one of His chosen flock, to steal pelts, even to provide a daughter's dowry and marriage, even from an evil Polish count who has hounded and robbed us all these years and would never even miss the loss.

" 'If that's the way it is,' I said to myself, 'I am quits with Him. I don't want to be one of His 'Chosen People' any longer!'

"I made my way home, entered the house, and found the evening meal on the table.

"My wife greeted me: 'Berel, wash your hands and come to the table.'

"Angrily, I refused to wash my hands. I sat down, took a piece of bread, and did not say the blessing. I ate well, and did not say grace. Afterwards, I did not repeat the evening service.

I went to bed, and did not say the *Shema.* The next morning I continued my rebellion. No prayers, no blessings. So the days passed. When the time for selichot came, I did not answer the call of the shamash in the early dawn to go to the synagogue, nor did I go to the synagogue on Rosh Hashanah—not even to hear the shofar. I could not forgive Him for what He had done to me.

"But when at last the holy day arrived, the Day of Atonement, I began to think: perhaps today I should forgive Him, for does He not forgive us too on Yom Kippur? But only on one condition: that He forgive everything, even the sins of mine which Yom Kippur does not atone for, for it is written that Yom Kippur atones for the sins man commits against God, but not that which he commits against his fellow man. If He will forgive everything, then I am willing to forgive Him, too. But if not, I too will not forgive.

"Tell me, Rabbi, which of us is right?"

"You are, Berel; you are," answered Levi Yitzhak with great joy. "You are right, and the judgment is hereby rendered in your favor. Let Him forgive *everything.*"

With that, Rabbi Levi Yitzhak began the Kol Nidre.

Hallah, Honey, and Apples

This Rosh Hashana meal for six blends the traditional with the contemporary. Begin the meal with pieces of apple and hallah dipped in honey. The sweet beginning signifies a sweet new year to come. The hallah here also symbolizes the cycle of the new year with its roundness. Some families add ladders or birds to the top of their hallah to commemorate the prayers rising to heaven.

Eating fish, especially the head of a fish, is another old tradition. Other foods that are commonly eaten during Rosh Hashana are honey cakes, taiglach (honey pastries), and carrot tzimmes, the last because the Yiddish word for "carrots" is *meyrin,* which means "to increase," with the idea of increasing one's privileges from God. There are numerous variations for all these recipes.

MENU
FAMILY DINNER FOR EIGHT
◆
Apples and Hallah Dipped in Honey
◆
Tzimmes
◆
Green Beans
◆
Honey Cake
◆
Taiglach

Round Hallah

1 package dry yeast
½ cup warm water
4 cups flour
1 cup hot water
2 tablespoons vegetable oil
½ tablespoon salt
2 tablespoons sugar (or less, to taste)
3 eggs, beaten

Preheat the oven to 350° F.

Dissolve the yeast in the warm water. Set aside. In a large mixing bowl, make a well in the flour. Set aside.

In another large bowl, pour in the hot water, followed by the oil, salt, and sugar. When the sugar has dissolved and the liquid mixture has cooled to lukewarm, add the yeast. Then add two eggs, beaten; mix thoroughly. Add the flour to the yeast mixture, half a cup or so at a time.

Turn out onto a lightly floured surface and knead well, adding flour if necessary for handling. Place the dough in a well-greased mixing bowl, cover with a clean towel or cloth, and let rise for about 2 hours (the dough should double in size). Knead again and form into a round shape.

Place on a greased and lightly floured baking pan. Let rise 25 minutes. Combine the yolk of the remaining egg with 1 teaspoon of cold water and mix well. Brush this mixture on the top of the challah. Bake for 10 to 15 minutes at 400° F, then at 350° F for another 45 minutes.

Variation: Add ½ cup raisins to the dough.

Tzimmes

1 onion
3 to 4 pounds boneless brisket
2 tablespoons schmaltz or vegetable oil
4 large carrots
1 lemon
4 medium sweet potatoes
3 large new potatoes
16 dried prunes
Boiling water
3 tablespoons juice from fresh orange
1 to 1½ tablespoons brown sugar
1 to 1½ tablespoons flour
Salt to taste
Freshly ground pepper to taste

Preheat oven to 350° F.

Slice the onion and brown it and the meat in the fat in a heavy skillet on top of the stove. Place the meat and the onion in a large roasting pan with cover.

Wash the carrots, peeling them if desired, and cut into thick coins. Cut the lemon into thin slices. Peel potatoes and cut into chunks. Place the carrots, prunes, lemon, sweet potatoes, and white potatoes around the meat in the roasting pan.

Combine two cups of boiling water with the orange juice and set aside. Mix together the brown sugar and flour in equal amounts, adding more or less for the desired amount of

sweetness. Add just enough plain hot water to the sugar-flour mixture to make a watery paste, then add this to the orange juice mixture. Stir well and pour over the meat, fruit, and vegetables. Add more boiling water to the roasting pan to cover the brisket and other ingredients. Cover and bake for 4 hours. Uncover and bake for 30 minutes more. The meat should be well browned.

Green Beans

1 pound green beans

2 tablespoons margarine

Juice of ½ lemon

Wash the beans and snip off the ends. Steam the green beans with boiling water for about 15 or 20 minutes. (Drop the beans into a steamer that is above the boiling water. Cover the pan and wait. Steaming brings out the color of the beans.) Drain, put into the serving bowl. Put dabs of the butter on top, squeeze the lemon juice over the beans, mix, and serve.

Taiglach

3 eggs

2 teaspoons vegetable oil

2 teaspoons sugar

½ teaspoon ginger

½ teaspoon baking powder

1½ to 2 cups flour

2 cups chopped pecans or other nutmeats

⅓ cup raisins, optional

Beat the eggs until light. Beat in the oil, then add the sugar gradually, mixing well after each addition. Add the ginger, baking powder and enough flour to make a manageable but not sticky dough. Knead until the dough is smooth, then roll into a long, narrow strip about ⅓-inch thick and cut pieces about ⅔-inch long.

Syrup

1 cup honey

¾ cup sugar

2 teaspoons ginger

Preheat the oven to 350° F.

Bring the honey and sugar to a low boil in a heavy pan. Pour the syrup into a low-sided baking pan. Add the pieces of dough one at a time. Turn them in the syrup before putting the pan in the oven. Bake for 20 to 25 minutes without opening the oven door. Add the nuts and stir or shake the pan to keep the dough pieces somewhat separate. Cook for another 15 minutes, or until golden and crisp, which may take an additional 10 minutes. Wet a wooden board with cold water and turn the taiglach onto the wet board. Dip hands in cold water and form the taiglach into 2-inch pieces. The honey should form a crust.

Honey Cake

3 cups sifted flour

1 teaspoon baking soda

2 teaspoons baking powder

2 teaspoons lemon zest

Pinch of cloves

1 teaspoon ginger

1 teaspoon cinnamon

½ teaspoon nutmeg

½ teaspoon salt

3 eggs

1 cup sugar

1 cup liquid honey

1 cup boiled black coffee

2 tablespoons oil and/or melted shortening

½ cup slivered almonds

Preheat the oven to 350° F.

Sift flour, baking powder, baking soda, lemon zest, spices, and salt together. Set aside.

Beat eggs until thick and light, about 5 minutes. Add sugar gradually and beat well. Add the honey, then the coffee and the shortening; blend well. Add the dry ingredients to the egg-honey mixture. Beat until well blended. Sprinkle nuts on the bottom of a loaf pan that has been greased and lined with parchment paper. Bake at 350° F for 35 to 40 minutes. Let stand for 5 minutes. Turn out on rack.

Rosh Hashana Cards

Materials:
Practice paper for card & envelope
patterns: newsprint or drawing paper
Card stock: Rice paper, watercolor paper,
construction paper
Envelope stock: Heavier watercolor paper
Card trims: Household aluminum foil, art
foil, colored tissue paper
Writing materials: Pencil, calligraphy pen,
watercolor or permanent ink markers
White household liquid glue or gluestick
Ruler

Before Beginning
A visit to an art store will provide a wealth
of paper choices for you. Increased interest
in handmade papers has caused dealers to
stock many different fibers, textures, and
colors in a wide range of prices. Watercolor
papers and construction papers also come
in many colors and textures. You will want
to select a paper that will form a crease
without cracking, and, if you are not going
to use a second layer of smooth paper for
your written messages, you'll want to have
on hand card stock that is compatible with
your choice of writing instruments.

Sample the flow of ink, and practice your
alphabet characters, on scrap pieces of your
good card papers. If the ink spreads out too
much because you've chosen a very porous
type of paper, lightly glue a smoother textured paper to the card front. It will serve as
both a firm base for your calligraphy and
add a subtle three-dimensional effect when
your designs are glued in place.

Likewise, test how the glue reacts with
the paper by gluing sample pieces. In any
case, with special art papers, always use the
glue very sparingly. Take note that you do
not let the glue ooze out of the edges or drip
onto the plain surfaces, since it will often
change the color of the paper. It's best to
glue by using just a small drop at the corners of the shapes.

Deciding on a Card Size
Remember that if you are going to send
your cards through the Postal Service, the
U.S. Post Office minimum first-class letter
size is 3½″ x 5″. If you mail a card that is
smaller, it will be returned to you for placement in a larger envelope. Also, if your card
is unusually thick, there will be a surcharge
for the special handling required.

It's more practical to stay within standard
measurements. We have suggested a 5″ x
6½″ card. This is large enough to give you a
good surface for laying out your design and
can be positioned either horizontally or ver-
tically.

Making Your Cards
Use newsprint or drawing paper to try out a
sample card size, or follow our directions for
a finished card size of 5″ x 6½″. With a
satisfactory size chosen, proceed to cut and
fold your art papers for the actual cards.

Because we have used a delicate rice
paper for our examples, we've started with
a paper that is 9½″ x 13″. Fold it in half
(illus. 1A), and then in half again, arriving at
the finished 5″ x 6½″ card in a double
thickness.

If you are using handmade papers, like
rice papers, notice that there are textured
edges formed by the papermaking process.
Try to keep one of the textured edges rough
on the 13-inch side of the card. When
folded, this edge will produce a very attractive effect.

Now that you have the actual card size
prepared, you can either decorate the card
as it is, or add a second texture of paper for
a more sophisticated design. We've lightly
glued the bottom edge of a strip of envelope
stock to the front of the card and folded it
over the edge so that it continues inside,
where the opposite edge is also lightly
glued. On the card positioned horizontally,
with the folded edge at the top, this makes
another writing surface on the inside of the
card (illus. 1B).

To decorate, assemble your trimming papers and cut motifs, such as the Star-of-
David. You might make a three-dimensional
Star-of-David by cutting out equilateral triangles of different sizes, and stacking them
up on the card. We used 1¾″, 2½″, and
3¼″ triangles of foil and tissue paper. In
addition, the overlapping tissue papers create new colors. Use just a dot of glue in the
center of the triangles. Or, for heavier papers, use a dot of glue on the corners.

Use a pencil and ruler to lightly draw
guidelines for the bottom edge of your let-
tering. Letter your messages. Let ink dry
thoroughly. Lightly erase guidelines, taking
care not to erode the surface texture of the
paper.

Making Your Envelopes
If you have chosen to make cards that are
5″ x 6½″, proceed to measure an envelope
pattern from newsprint or inexpensive
drawing paper, according to illus. 1C. This is

probably the simplest style of envelope to
work with. Cut it out and fold on the dotted
lines to create your envelope. It should be
slightly larger than your card. If the size is
right, trace the pattern onto your envelope
art paper. Cut it out and crease on the
dotted lines, using a ruler, if necessary, to
make a smooth crease.

Apply glue lightly to the outer edges of
the bottom flap (illus. 1D) and fold up the
bottom. When you are ready to mail your
card, use a thin line of white glue on the top
flap to seal, or use sealing wax.

If you've chosen to make cards of a
different size, use our example to make a
pattern for your own envelope. First trace
the shape of the card in the center of a sheet
of newsprint, making it slightly larger.
Then, add the top, bottom and side flaps to
match the proportions of your own card
size. Fold on the dotted lines and check to
see that the envelope pieces are the right
size. Adjust, and trace your pattern onto
your envelope art paper. Complete envelope as described above.

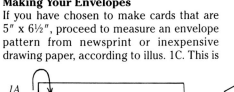

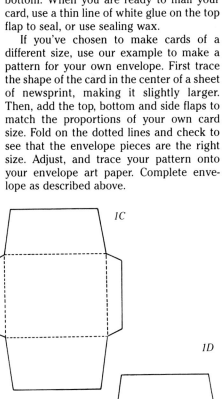

SUKKOT

The Harvest Festival

"On the fifteenth day of this seventh month (five days after Yom Kippur) the festival of Sukkot (shall be celebrated) seven days unto the Lord...." (Leviticus 23:34–36)

In the wake of the sound of the shofar, the solemnity of the High Holyday season shifts from the sublime to the celebratory. The festival of Sukkot, also known as the "Feast of Booths," marks this joyous transition as the autumnal holiday season draws to a close.

The Cycle and the Sukkah

Sukkot commemorates another cycle as well. The people of Israel escaped from Egypt (Passover), entered into a covenant with God at Mount Sinai (Shavuot), and wandered about the desert encamped in portable, thatched huts, eagerly awaiting entrance into Canaan. In Exodus, Leviticus, and again in Deuteronomy, Sukkot is named as the third and final festival in this process of the Exodus from Egypt.

Each member of this biblical trilogy (Passover, Shavuot, Sukkot) shares a common distinction in the tradition. In the days of the Temple, Jews would make a pilgrimage to Jerusalem three times a year, bringing sacrifices for the Holy Temple. Even today, all three festivals are marked by home observance and special synagogue worship such as reciting the Hallel (a selection of psalms designated for festivals), reading a special portion from the Torah, and participating in the _mussaf_ service (recalling the special sacrifices that were brought to the Temple on that day). But each festival also generates its own customs and traditions which combine to give an individual flavor and personality to that day. Sukkot instinctively conjures up notions of the sukkah, the Four Species (_Arba'ah Minim_), and the special celebration motif. The tradition as a whole becomes the sum total of its independent parts.

Sukkot extends for nine days. The first two days and the last two are major festival days while the five intermediate days assume a secondary level of observance. In Israel, only eight days are observed, and the larger festival is observed only on the first and last days. The _sukkah,_ which literally means "covering" or "shelter," is the focal point of the festival. (_Sukkot_ is the plural form of sukkah.)

Historically, the Israelites traversed the Sinai desert camping in these temporary dwelling units.

In sukkot shall every Israelite dwell for seven days. So that the generations will know that [I caused] the children of Israel to dwell in sukkot when I removed them from Egypt. (Leviticus 23)

Symbolically, this verse raises the theme of impermanence. The picture of escaped, desert-bound slaves, bearing their homes on their backs, never sleeping a week in the same site, drives home the image of a precarious existence and the message that all life is only a temporary arrangement.

Primarily, Sukkot observance calls for dwelling in a sukkah for seven days. While _dwelling_ means eating and sleeping, most people of temperate climates limit their activity to eating and study. Some, however, do choose to include a sleeping bag or a mattress in their sukkah. The other essential ingredient of proper holiday observance is sharing meals with others. Hospitality is a basic element of the festival. In addition to Sukkot, the name _Chag Ha'asif_—Festival of the Ingathering—is also used by the Bible. As a harvest time festival, Sukkot has taken on many qualities of a holiday of thanksgiving. Our sukkah and our meal are the horn of plenty we share with all.

Another fundamental factor of Sukkot is the joy of celebration of a people united by a shared heritage. The Bible, in prescribing "happiness," specifically in conjunction with Sukkot, conferred upon the festival yet another title: _Z'man Simchatainu_—time of our joy.

Sukkot can vary depending on climate, budget, and ability. The variety shown here represent the extremes—from apartment balcony enclosures to primitive, desert, open-to-breezes huts.

The Essentials of a Sukkah

Picture a large toolshed. Instead of a roof, imagine long, one-inch by two-inch wooden slats extending from side to side of the shed. Cover these slats with greenery or detached foliage. Add some dining furniture, decorate to taste, and you've got a functioning sukkah that will serve as many people as you can feed.

To build a sukkah, you need not erect a monumental edifice. Any lightweight material sturdy enough to withstand average regional winds will do. Sukkot range from canvas, to wood, to aluminum, to fiberglass.

The walls of a sukkah should not exceed 35 feet (960 cm.) in height nor should they be shorter than 35 inches (80 cm.). The sukkah should not be more than 10 to 12 inches (24 cm.) off the ground. The most important part of the sukkah is the roofing. You must lay a frame and a covering that allows you to see through to the sky. Sparse wooden slats are fine, and any green shrubbery or foliage, will do. Windows and electrical wiring can be useful additions, and often, the use of one or even two outside walls of a house can significantly reduce material costs.

Building a sukkah can be a fun family affair. The eldest family members may want to string apples and gourds to hang as decorations, while the youngest can make cranberry strings to liven up the sukkah. Pinning up collected new year's cards, posters available at your local Hebrew bookstore, and even party decorations such as plastic streamers and crepe paper (for when it doesn't rain) can generate an air of excitement and anticipation for the sumptuous meal that family and friends will share together in the sukkah.

These delicacies, above, are commonly served at Sukkot. At right, a young girl adds decorations to the sukkah.

The Four Species

Of the other symbols used in the celebration of Sukkot, the most prominent is the Four Species.

> And you shall take for yourselves on the first day (of Sukkot) the fruit of a goodly tree, a palm branch, the myrtle branch, and the willow of the brook; and you shall rejoice before the Lord your God seven days. (Leviticus 23)

The fruit of a goodly tree is the citron, the etrog; the palm branch is known as the lulav; the myrtle is called the hadas; and the willow is known as the aravah. Through these four species, the joy of Sukkot is sustained even outside the sukkah.

Acquisition of a lulav and etrog set is not a major undertaking. If you happen to live in New York City, take a stroll through the Lower East Side of Manhattan the day after Yom Kippur. You'll probably find a lulav and etrog to suit your fancy. You'll also see the excitement generated by the many vendors both indoors and out multiplied by the throngs of people coming to buy. If Canal and Delancey are not within reach, many synagogues take orders for ready-made sets, buying them from distributors either in Israel, New York, or locally. If you're fortunate enough to live in a community that supports a Hebrew bookstore, it may also be able to accommodate your needs.

Part of the specialness of Sukkot stems from the emphasis on beauty. The tradition hails subjective aesthetics as integral to the celebration. When buying your own lulav and etrog, you have the luxury of choosing each of the four species to suit your taste. The lulav and etrog must be beautiful, _hadar._ And once objective criteria are met, beauty falls to the eye of the consumer.

In purchasing an etrog, look for one that is clean and free of spots and leaf marks. Most etrogim grow with a stem as well as a tip, a crown. This crown must remain intact. Once these basics are established, the more subjective factors such as size and shape come into question. Some like their etrogim rounder, while others prefer theirs more elongated. Generally, a rippled texture is preferred in contrast to the smoothness of a lemon. An indented stem may be thought of as nicer than one that protrudes. A wide base narrowing up toward the tip makes for a lovely shape. Check for ripeness. Very yellow means very ripe. You're better off buying a green etrog than a very yellow one. Your etrog will ripen quickly, and you can always hasten the ripening process by placing an apple or two next to it. In this way you can control the color to your liking.

The citron (etrog), _the palm branch_ (lulav), _the myrtle_ (hadas), _and the willow_ (aravah) _comprise the Four Species_ (Arb'ah Minim). **When the etrog is not being used, it should be placed in a special container such as the ones shown** below right.

A lulav should be as green and as erect as possible. Take care that the leaves remain intact and that the center spinal leaf does not split. Height is a matter of personal taste, but lulavim four feet and over get a bit unwieldly. You will want three myrtle branches twelve to fifteen inches in length. The most attractive branches are fresh and lush, with medium-sized leaves and few berries. The two willow branches should be taller than the myrtle, with narrow, smooth, elongated leaves. Once you have chosen, bind the myrtle and willow to the lulav with a rubber band, a piece of string, or a loose palm leaf. In observing the ritual, take the lulav in the right hand, with the etrog in the left, while reciting the prescribed blessing.

The group of psalms known as Hallel is sung on all festive holidays, Sukkot included. The lulav and etrog are taken up in the rejoicing and song throughout the Hallel service. They are again taken in hand at the end of the mussaf service for the *Hoshanot*. This processional, at which the entire congregation circles the sanctuary, also contains hymns of joy and thanksgiving. Another celebration of Sukkot recalls the ancient commemoration of the water libations at the Temple. Even today, many *Yeshivot* (schools of study), especially in Israel, sponsor a *Simchat Bet Hashoaivah*, a party, at which music and dance affirm that ancient practice.

**Reading the Torah at the Wailing Wall,** _above. **The cycle of Torah readings ends**_
**on Simchat Torah,** _right, **the ninth day of**_ _**Sukkot. A new cycle begins immediately.**_

The Last Days

The seventh day of Sukkot is known as Hoshana Rabba. The special synagogue service shares several elements with the High Holydays. The cantor wears solemn white garb and the service is chanted in the melody of the austere and the sublime. Other customs include an extended Hoshanot service—seven processions instead of one, and the beating of the willow branch at the end of the service.

Although it marks the eighth day of Sukkot, Shemini Atzeret is an independent festival with its own biblical source. We chant the prayer for rain as Israel anticipates the winter season (as opposed to summer, the dry season). Shemini Atzeret also marks the last official day of Sukkot, and we therefore offer our reluctant farewell to the sukkah.

On the ninth day of the Sukkot festival, we celebrate Simchat Torah, proclaiming our completion of the cycle of reading the Torah. On this day we read the final passages from Deuteronomy and immediately recommence the cycle. This annual commencement calls for singing and dancing both at night and in the morning. All participate in the festivities. In many communities, celebrations continue throughout the night, often including dancing in the streets. During the day worshipers, especially children, are called to the Torah so that all can participate actively in the cycle, in its renewal, and in its preservation.

The festival of Sukkot indeed lives up to the responsibility assumed by its chronological placement in the calendar. Its position as anchor on two accounts (in the biblical series of festivals and in the High Holyday series) suggests a holiday of paramount significance and scope. Simchat Torah, its end, looks to the Torah as the perennial mainstay of the Jewish tradition recalling its rich past while acting as guarantor for its future. The sukkah stresses our vulnerability by removing us from the security of our permanent homes, and leaving us open under the stars. In our self-imposed exile, we are reminded of the mutual dependence of mankind, and the joy that the simple harmony of a family together and a meal shared with others can bring.

From *The Four Species*

By Yaacov Luria

It all begins in the Zlotchevsky orchard in Rishon L'Tzion, South of Jaffa. After twenty-nine years of growth, the citron trees are a bit over ten feet tall. Before the autumn rains begin in late October, Yussi cultivates, fertilizes and prunes his trees. If all goes well, by the following July the fruit is mature enough to pick.

"Now Yussi is working like ten horses," says Mordecai. "He goes to Safed in Galilee to find the best myrtle. In Israel the myrtle is a tree, not a flower. Then he cuts palm branches—hundreds and hundreds of them. Now he must gather everything to be shipped. The citrons—only the best—are wrapped in boxes. The palm branches are stacked in wooden frames. The myrtle must be kept moist and refrigerated, or they dry up. Everything is ready? So thank God for El-Al. The whole business flies 5,000 miles to New York, and Nehama and I shlepp along too."

What about the willows? "Willows grow in America—the only one of the *arba minim* not imported. As long as the twigs are red and the leaves have smooth edges, it's a kosher aravah," Mordecai explains.

The visitor calls Mordecai's attention to a blond, heavyset young man who is examining an etrog with a magnifying glass. At times he holds it up to the sunlight in the doorway and gently tries to dislodge with a tooth pick what looks like a tiny speck of soil.

"A very particular customer," notes Mordecai. "He will pay much more than the thirteen dollars we get for the cheapest etrog and lulav. He comes early and takes his time. Closer to the holiday he could buy cheaper." Then why not come later? "Ah, by then the best would be already sold."

What is "the best"? Mordecai hefts a citron in his upraised palm. "See, how it has mounds and pits—like hills and valleys on the earth. It pleases the eye, but more still, it has a personality that belongs to itself alone. It has hadar. In English you translate hadar as 'goodly,' yes? 'The fruit of goodly trees.' But in Hebrew, what a word is hadar! It means beauty, majesty, splendor, glory, magnificence, radiance. Ah, how I wish I knew better English to tell you what lies in the word hadar!"

The visitor thinks that Mordecai's verbal performance itself is an example of hadar. But Mordecai is not content until he tells a parable from the Midrash. The four species are likened to the four kinds of Jews: The etrog, at the summit, with both a good taste and a pleasant smell, symbolizes the Jew who has both learning and good deeds. At the bottom is the aravah, the willow that neither tastes nor smells good, which suggests the Jew without either learning or good deeds. In between are the lulav with taste but no scent—the Jew with learning but not good deeds—and the myrtle with scent but no taste—the Jew who is virtuous but ignorant. But all four types, says Mordecai, are needed to make a balanced community. How terrible if everyone were a learned *tzaddik* (or saint)!

All at once the visitor sees the young man with the magnifying glass and the tooth pick in a new light. What has just now seemed petty and overfussy emerges as a tradition-hallowed search for perfection. To sing hosannahs to God one must wave heavenwards a palm branch and a citron of singular beauty.

The visitor has come only to observe and satisfy his curiosity. Moved now by an imprecise and vaguely understood urge, he asks Mordecai and Nehama to select an etrog and lulav for him to carry home. They need not be perfect examples of their kind, he adds, just beautiful enough to qualify as hadar.

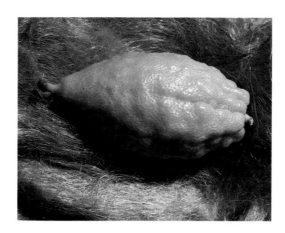

Sisu Ve-simhu

Si —— -su ve - sim hu — -be-sim hat To - rah - ut' - nu — ka — -vod — la - To -

rah —— - ki tov — -sah — -rah — mi — -kol se - ho - rah. Mi -

Fine

paz u - mit - ni - nim — - ye - ka - rah. Na - gil —— - ve - na - sis na -

gil — - ve - na - sis be - zot — - ha - To - rah — - ha - To - rah —— Ki

D.S. al Fine

hi - la - nu oz, ki hi - la - nu oz oz oz ve - o — - ra. Si -

Sisu Ve-simhu

Rejoice and be happy on Simchat Torah
And give honor to the Torah.
For its merchandise is better than any other.
It is more precious than fine gold or pearls.
Let us exult and rejoice in this Torah,
For it is for us strength and light.

Translation by LARRY KWASS

Hallel

Here is the myrtle;
once the Promised Land untended.
Rendering
what the eyes see that
Can't be taught
except by vision.

Sweet, yet tasting naught
naughtless.

(Words appearing willow-pure
in sluices of life unknown
yet meaning

anything in rhetoric
if mounted
and bending into musical staves
each year harvested
more abstract.)

Gold of the sun-heart
orbited by countless resolutions—

tart to tongue
and throat, constructing in time

this scaffolding
the noble spine—

sprouting out of the dust
like a date-palm: succulent,
divine.

Take it; take the whole bouquet
and shake it in all four corners

of the earth. Z'man simhatenu.
Again and again

wrapping yourselves in
its miracles
those scarves so
subtly fringed
at the border.
—CAROL ADLER

Bounty From the Harvest

MENU
LIGHT DINNER FOR FOUR
◆
Hallah Dipped in Honey
◆
Borscht
◆
Fillet of Sole with Apples and Mushrooms
◆
Harvest Pie

Fresh fruits and nuts abound during the days of Sukkot. Sukkot are decorated with apples, pears, grapes, peppers, gourds, pumpkins, and corn. These same ingredients can also make a sumptuous meal. The menus here draw from the harvest bounty but are simple and contained; they can easily be carried from kitchen to sukkah.

Hallah dipped in honey is a common sight at Sukkot, too, but not as much as it is during Rosh Hashana. Stuffed cabbage or stuffed grape leaves, tzimmes, strudel, baclava, and kreplach are all traditional foods in various parts of the world during these days of joyous celebration.

Borscht

6 medium beets
5 cups water
Salt to taste
Sugar to taste
Juice of half a lemon
1 egg
4 to 5 stalks scallions
1 cucumber
2 new potatoes
1 cup sour cream

Peel beets and cut into small sticks. Cook in salted water until tender. Add sugar and lemon juice. Simmer for 10 to 15 minutes.

Beat egg in large bowl, then add beet mixture. Stir thoroughly. Chill.

Cut scallions for garnish. Peel and dice cucumber for garnish. Boil new potatoes until tender and cut into chunks for garnish. Serve with a dollop of sour cream.

Sole Fillets with Apples and Mushrooms

8 large fresh mushrooms
1 lemon
1 to 2 cloves garlic, to taste
6 sole fillets
5 tablespoons unsalted butter
1 teaspoon lemon juice
White pepper to taste
2 or 3 tart apples
6 sprigs fresh tarragon
1 tablespoon shallots

Preheat oven to 350° F.

Clean the mushrooms and slice thinly. Cut the lemon in two and sprinkle some of the lemon juice on the mushrooms. Set aside. Mince the garlic and set aside. Rinse the fish fillets, pat them dry, and place each on a piece of cooking parchment large enough to fold over and seal. Sprinkle each fillet with the remaining juice of the cut lemon, then set aside.

Melt 2 tablespoons of the butter over moderate heat and saute the mushrooms for one minute. Add the lemon juice and pepper and cook another 2 minutes. Spoon equal portions of the mushrooms onto the fish fillets. In the same skillet, melt 1 tablespoon of butter, then add the apples; saute for 2 minutes, stirring constantly. Arrange equal portions of the apples on top of the mushrooms. Place the remaining butter in the pan to melt, then add the tarragon, garlic, and shallots. Saute the shallots until tender. Spoon the tarragon mixture over the apples.

Seal the parchment packages by folding on the diagonal. Roll the edges to make a half-moon shape. Place the packaged fish on a baking sheet and bake for 20 minutes. Slit the packages and serve while steaming hot.

Harvest Pie

2 cups all-purpose flour
⅔ cups chilled unsalted butter, cubed
6 tablespoons ice water

In a large bowl, combine the flour and salt. Cut in the butter until the mixture separates into pea-sized pieces. Add one tablespoon of water to a small area of the flour mixture; toss gently with a fork and push aside. Add another tablespoon of water to a different area of the flour mixture, and repeat until the dough barely masses together. (Add up to one more tablespoon water if necessary.) Divide the dough in two and gently gather each piece into a ball. Wrap well and refrigerate for about 45 minutes; the dough should be chilled but still malleable. Roll one ball out onto a lightly floured surface. Preheat the oven to 400°F. Fit the rolled crust into a 9-inch pie pan, easing the dough into the sides of the pan with the sides of your fingers. Trim and leave a 1-inch edge.

Place a sheet of foil on top of the dough and add enough beans or pie weights to prevent the crust from heaving. Bake the crust for 8 minutes. Remove from the oven and set aside while preparing the filling.

Filling

4 cups fresh fruit (apples, peaches, and firm pears)
½ to 1 cup sugar
1 teaspoon grated lemon zest
⅛ teaspoon cardamom
⅛ teaspoon ground cloves
Pinch ground ginger
1¾ tablespoons butter
1 tablespoon sugar
½ tablespoon cinnamon

Pare, core, and slice the apples. Pit and slice the peaches. Core and slice the pears. Set the fruit aside in a large bowl. Combine the sugar, lemon zest, cardamom, cloves, and ginger, and sprinkle over the fruit; mix gently. Brush the bottom of the pie shell with 1¾ tablespoon of the butter, melted. Mound the fruit in the pie shell and spread evenly. Preheat oven to 375°F. Roll out second crust and cover the pie, fluting the edges. Prick the crust in several places. Combine the sugar and cinnamon and sprinkle over the crust liberally or as desired. Bake for 30 to 35 minutes or until the pie is golden brown.

Stuffed Cabbage

1 large head of cabbage
2 to 3 medium onions
5 cloves garlic
4 stalks celery
1 red bell pepper
1 green bell pepper
½ cup fresh dill
2 tablespoons vegetable oil
2 eggs
1½ pounds lean ground beef
¼ to ½ teaspoon salt to taste
Freshly ground pepper to taste
¼ teaspoon ground cloves
1 teaspoon dried thyme
¼ cup bread crumbs
1 can (16 ounces) chopped tomatoes
1 can (10¾ ounces) chicken broth or 1 cup rich chicken stock
¼ cup dry sherry

Core the cabbage and discard the top few outer leaves. Boil enough water to cover the cabbage. Put the cabbage carefully into the hot water, and cook covered for approximately 12 minutes (longer if you want very soft leaves). Remove the head, plunge it into cold water, and drain.

Chop the onions, garlic, celery, peppers, and dill. Reserve approximately one-third of the onions, garlic, and dill to season the baking liquid. In a skillet, saute the larger portion of the onions and garlic in oil; after one minute add the celery and peppers, and cook until the onions are tender and translucent, about 5 minutes. Cool the vegetables until warm to the touch.

In a small bowl, beat the eggs slightly. Combine with the ground meat in a mixing bowl. Add the salt, pepper, cloves, thyme, and larger portion of the dill. Mix well. Add the bread crumbs and the warm vegetables. Mix by hand.

Preheat the oven to 375° F. Taking the cabbage leaves one by one, lay each out on the work surface so the leaves are curving upward. Spoon a heaping tablespoonful or more of the filling into each leaf. Fold the sides of the leaf over the filling and then fold the top down. Then fold the core end of the leaf down. Place seam side down in a large baking pan. The stuffed cabbages should fit in one layer in the pan.

Combine the tomatoes, chicken broth, and sherry. Pour over the stuffed cabbages. Then fill in the "holes" with the reserved onions, garlic, and dill. Salt and pepper to taste. Cook covered for 45 minutes. Remove cover and cook another 15 minutes. Spoon the cabbages out with a dollop of sauce on top.

Apple Cake

1½ cups flour
⅞ cups sugar
2 teaspoons baking powder
½ teaspoon cinnamon
¼ teaspoon allspice
Pinch of salt
1 egg, beaten
½ cup pareve milk
4 tablespoons pareve margarine, melted
1 teaspoon vanilla
4 or 5 tart apples, cut into chunks

Preheat oven to 350°F. Grease and lightly flour a bundt pan and set aside. Combine flour, sugar, baking powder, cinnamon, allspice, and salt; sift together and set aside. Combine the egg, pareve milk and margarine, and vanilla; mix well. Add the egg mixture to the dry ingredients; beat well by hand. Stir in approximately three quarters of the apples. Pour batter into the bundt pan and spread evenly around the ring. Sprinkle the remaining apples evenly on top of the batter. Bake for 30 minutes. Remove from the oven and cool on a rack. Remove from the pan and decorate by placing a paper doily on top of the cake, sprinkling confectioners' sugar on top, and then carefully removing the doily.
Variation: After adding the apples and before baking, sprinkle brown sugar over the batter. This will replace the confectioner's sugar topping.

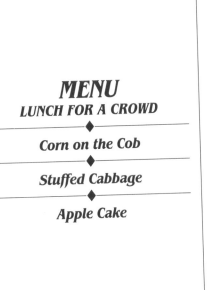

Festive Bouquet

Materials:
Rubrum lilies
Smaller, paler lilies
Caspia
Pink stock
White bouvardia
Brown stems
Tall, slim, glass vase

Begin by placing the bare branches at the proportional heights as shown in the photo- graph, *above left*. The brown stems become the mechanics of the design, securing and concealing the green stems of the lilies. Next, incorporate the smaller lilies and the caspia to lighten the overall look. Finally, add the bright pink stock, which brings boldness to the bouquet and completes the range of pinks. The white bouvardia con- tributes the perfect touch of variety, bal- ance, and unity.

CHANUKAH

The Festival of Lights

Chanukah, the Festival of Lights, is at once the best known and least known of the Jewish holidays. The customs of Chanukah, such as lighting the *menorah,* playing *dreidel,* eating potato latkes, and giving and getting Chanukah *gelt* and gifts are familiar to all its celebrants. The story behind the holiday, of how the menorah in the Holy Temple stayed lit for eight days with very little oil, is recounted each year as we light the Chanukah candles.

The events that led up to this miracle, however, as well as the historical setting of Chanukah, are often forgotten.

The Story Behind Chanukah

The story of Chanukah actually begins in the year 336 B.C.E.* when Alexander the Great conquered the Persian Empire, which included Judea (modern-day Israel). The Jews' relationship with Alexander was long and fruitful. He sponsored many sacrifices in the Temple. Alexander promised the Jews that his empire would not interfere with their religious practices both in Judea and in the diaspora, and he exempted the Jews from the royal tribute during the Sabbatical year. The Jews were also invited to participate in the Greek army, which shows that their loyalties were not suspect.

Alexander requested, as was the custom, that his statue be placed on the Temple mount as a symbol of Jewish loyalty to the Empire. The Jews, with their strong aversion to graven images, demurred, but offered instead to name all their first-born male children Alexander.

After the death of Alexander, Judea fell under the rule of the Ptolemies of Alexandria. During this period, many of the Jews were influenced by the ideas of Hellenism and began to assimilate into the Greek culture. It was at this time that King Ptolemy, to promote a better understanding of the Jews, commissioned the famous Greek translation of the Bible commonly known as the Septuagint.

Later, the Ptolemaic Empire of Egypt and the Seleucid Empire of Syria fought bitterly to gain control over Judea, because it was a strategic location, the gateway between the continents of Africa and Asia. Finally the Seleucids won. By this time a sizable minority of the Jews were thoroughly Hellenized. Forsaking the ways of their fathers, they adopted the Greek fashion of dress, and the Greek language and philosophies. They looked upon their nonassimilated brethren as holdouts to a set of antiquated traditions. These Hellenists tried to influence the others, sometimes going as far as antagonizing the rulers against the traditionalists.

The Jews' most pressing problem was their ruler, Antiochus IV Epiphanes, who was considered an unstable man. The historian Polybius wrote that Antiochus behaved erratically, in no ways befitting a king. He would occasionally go through the streets giving away money, and he enjoyed spilling oil on the floor of the bathhouse and watching people fall. In fact, his people

Al Hanism: A Chanukah Prayer

For all the miracles and for the salvation and for the victories and for the battles that You performed for our fathers years ago at this time, we thank You.

In the time of Mattathias the son of Jochanon the High Priest and his sons—when the evil Seleucid kingdom rose up against Your people Israel to make them forget your Laws and to lead them away from Your will, You in Your abundant mercy stood up for them in their time of need. You delivered the strong into the hands of the weak, the many into the hands of the few, the wicked into the hands of the righteous. And for Your people Israel You caused a great victory and salvation on this day. Then they turned to Your Sanctuary and cleansed Your Temple and relit the lights in Your Holy Courtyard. And they established these eight days of Chanukah in order to thank and to praise Your great name.

nicknamed him *Epimanes*, which means "madman." Antiochus claimed that he came in peace to Jerusalem in 168 B.C.E., but instead, he plundered the money used for upkeep from the storehouses of the Holy Temple and then pillaged the city and took 10,000 captives, mostly women and children to be sold into slavery. Antiochus and his army burned, sacked and looted, and killed anyone who opposed them. But the greatest affront of all was that on the 25th of Kislev, 168 B.C.E., Antiochus entered the Holy Temple, erected a statue of Zeus Olympus on the altar of burnt offerings and sacrificed a swine upon it. He then took the blood and splattered it within the Holy of Holies.

Antiochus, devoted to the political and cultural ideas of Hellenism, did not want to kill the Jews. He only wanted to introduce them to the Greek culture and break them of a "backward" religion. Everywhere the Greek armies went, the people embraced Hellenism and gladly became part of the widespread Greek culture, but not the Jews. Insulted, Antiochus enacted a number of anti-Jewish decrees. He prohibited proper Temple worship and compelled the Jews to build altars and make sacrifices to the Greek gods. He forced the Jews to desecrate the Sabbath, and he forbade circumcision. The Greeks accepted the practice of many other laws of the Torah, which were similar to Hellenic customs, but these few commandments were in direct contradiction to the philosophies of the Greeks. Sacrificing in the Temple demonstrated the Jews' loyalty to the one God of Heaven. Likewise, observing the Sabbath showed that

the Jews acknowledged God as the Creator of the world, which went against the Greek belief that the world was eternal. And circumcision, the sacred covenant between the Jews and God, ran counter to the Greeks' notion of the human body as the ultimate expression of perfection in nature. The Greeks celebrated the body through sculpture, painting, and athletics. Many a Hellenized Jew took great pains to hide his circumcision from his Greek friends at the *Gymnasium* who viewed it as a desecration of the body.

These decrees caused great anguish for the Jews. Some complied. Many, particularly the women, refused to comply. And some openly disobeyed the King's edicts. Chana, a woman who chose to disobey, had seven sons, and together they publicly denounced the harsh policies of Antiochus. Antiochus arrested them all and offered each son the choice of eating swine-flesh or death. One by one, each son refused to violate their fundamental law and was tortured and killed in front of the others. After each death, Antiochus gave the survivors the chance to renounce their ways and pledge allegiance to the Greek ruler. The family refused. Finally Antiochus came to the youngest son, a mere child. Thinking to trick the boy into bowing before him worshipfully, Antiochus threw his signet ring in front of his throne and asked the boy to pick it up. The boy responded that he would do nothing that could even be construed by an onlooker as an act of worshiping the King. Enfuriated, Antiochus had the child slain. Chana, who had witnessed all seven deaths, uttered a prayer

thanking God for allowing her to live to see her children die sanctifying God's name rather than renouncing the religion of their fathers, before she too was slain by the Greek guards.

The story of their martyrdom spread quickly throughout Judea. The cruel execution of Chana and her sons became a symbol of the evil oppression of Antiochus and his armies. Tensions mounted. In the town of Modi'im, about eight miles outside of Jerusalem, an elderly *cohain* (priest) named Mattathias witnessed a Hellenist offering a pig on an altar in the village square. Enraged, Mattathias unsheathed his dagger and killed the man. At first, everyone was stunned. Then Mattathias cried out, "Whoever is for God and His Law, follow me!" Mattathias, joined by his five loyal sons and a small group of brave rebels, fled into the hills. The revolution had begun.

Once in the hills the band of guerillas appointed Judah Maccabee (Judas Maccabaeus), one of Mattathias' sons, as their leader. The Maccabees, as they were called, gathered arms and waited for the next battle.

They did not wait long. As soon as Antiochus had heard of Mattathias' revolt he mobilized the Jerusalem garrison to locate the rebels in the hills and crush the insurrection. The two troops clashed—the mighty Greek army against a ragtag band of revolutionaries. And then, the impossible happened. Placing all their trust in God, the Maccabees managed to defeat the Greeks and rout them from Jerusalem. This unbelievable military victory is one of the miracles of Chanukah and is the focus of the special Chanukah prayer "Al Hanisim" (see box on page 58).

Although the Jews were now free of the Greek oppression, they still had before them the mammoth task of repairing the damage done to the Holy Temple. The stones of the altar, defiled by the blood of hogs, were removed and hidden away. The walls and floors of the Temple were scrubbed clean and a new altar was erected. The Temple was finally ready. On the 25th of Kislev 165 B.C.E., exactly three years after it had been defiled by Antiochus, the Holy Temple was rededicated. When it came time to relight the menorah only one small jar of olive oil that had not been defiled by the Greeks could be found within the entire Temple. It would take an eight day round-trip journey to obtain new pure oil. But the High Priest, determined to rededicate the Temple even if the menorah could be kindled for only one day, lit the menorah. The next day, to everyone's amazement, the menorah was miraculously still lit. For eight days the oil burned, until a new supply of oil could be brought. The community rejoiced, thanking God for His favor.

The next year the leaders of Israel declared that every year on the 25th of Kislev the Jews should celebrate the miracle of *Chanukah* (which means "dedication") with prayers of thanksgiving for the military victory, the victory that God gave to the few and the weak and unskilled who believed in Him. The leaders also ordained the kindling of the lamps, one light for each night, in commemoration of the miracle in the Temple.

The Menorah

In earliest times, the Chanukah menorahs were merely small individual clay lamps. On each night of Chanukah, another lamp was added. Then, large circular lamps with eight openings for the wicks were used.

Originally the menorah was kept outside on the left side of the doorpost opposite the *mezuzah,* in order to publicize the miracle of Chanukah to the world. In the event of windy weather, glass lanterns were used. When the Jews were persecuted by pagan fire-worshipers in the diaspora for displaying the menorah, the rabbis permitted the menorah to be kindled indoors. Since the menorahs no longer had to contend with the elements, Jewish artisans began to explore the artistic possibilities of candelabra design.

The first new menorahs were small cups fashioned of silver or other metals and mounted in a line on a horizontal base. During the Middle Ages a back wall was added so that the menorah could be hung on the inside of the doorpost opposite the mezuzah. In France craftspeople made the back wall to resemble Gothic architecture. A French menorah might appear to have a miniature facade of the Cathedral of Notre Dame, including trefoils, Gothic rose windows, colonnades, and arches. In Spain menorahs incorporated Moslem design, the back walls commonly boasting Moorish arches. During the Renaissance in Italy, menorahs became more ornate; elaborate back walls often depicted biblical scenes.

In Germany the menorah followed the same evolution it did elsewhere, progressing from individual cups to mounted cups with a back wall. But from the Middle Ages to the eighteenth century the Chanukah menorah often took the form of a star-shaped hanging chandelier, which could be used for the Sabbath lamps.

In Iran and Iraq the Jews continued to use round lamps of stone and metal into the eighteenth century. Later they used standing menorahs of silver with glass cups for the oil. In poorer areas the individual cups used were made of brass, bronze, stone, or even clay.

Now mass-produced menorahs are most common, al-

though hand-crafted ones such as the stained-glass example by Nancy Golden are available (see "Useful Addresses' on page 156).

Chanukah is celebrated with prayers such as the "Al Hanisim" and the Hallel and with candle lighting. The candles are lit at night just after dark—one candle on the first night and another candle each night thereafter for eight nights in all. As one faces the menorah, the candles are inserted from right to left. An additional candle, called the *shamash* ("assistant"), is usually placed off to the side. The lighting of the candles with the shammash proceeds from left to right, starting with the candle for the newest night. The blessings are then recited, often followed by the singing of "Ma'oz Tzur." Written in the thirteenth century, the song describes how God has been the foundation of the Jewish people throughout history and how He has saved them countless times.

Everyone is obligated to light the Chanukah menorah. Not only men and women but children as well, as soon as they are capable of safely holding a lit candle. The sages put a special emphasis on the obligation of women to light, because tradition has it that it was partly through the actions of a valorous woman named Judith that the military victory of Chanukah took place.

The Story of Judith

Judith was a very righteous and extremely beautiful widow who lived in the town of Bethulia, which nestled in a mountain pass on the outskirts of Judea. When the troops of the general Holofernes approached, the Jews of Bethulia prepared for an ambush. Realizing what lay ahead, Holofernes laid seige to the town. Soon Bethulia's water supply was depleted and the elders of the town gave God an ultimatum: Let it rain or in five days the townspeople would surrender.

Judith rebuked the elders for challenging God and set off with her handmaiden to rectify the situation. She approached Holofernes' camp and told the guards that she had come to instruct Holofernes on how to defeat the Jews. Once inside Holofernes' tent, Judith began to seduce the general. She produced from her basket cheeses and jugs of wine, and they dined together. Owing to his lust for Judith and his thirst from the cheeses, Holofernes overindulged, became drunk from the wine, and fell soundly asleep. Grasping his sword from its sheath, Judith beheaded Holofernes and put his head in her basket. Leaving his tent, she proceeded back to her village and presented the head to the elders. The elders posted the head over the gates of the town. When the enemy troops realized that their great leader had been killed they fled in terror. The bravery of one woman saved thousands.

Fun and Games

Many Jews eat delicacies prepared from cheese on Chanukah. Also, because the miracle in the Temple involved oil, it is customary to eat foods fried in oil, such as potato latkes.

It is also customary to give children Chanukah _gelt,_ which was once given to children to pay their Hebrew teachers. Now gifts are exchanged, lending a festive air to the holiday. Since no work should be done while the candles are lit there is a long-standing tradition that the evenings of Chanukah be given over to fun and games. By the Middle Ages, many European Jews indulged in a yearly game of _Kvitlach,_ which resembles our card game of Twenty-one. The children also indulged in a little gambling of their own, playing dreidel for penny-ante stakes. Tradition has it that during the Greek occupation of Judea, Jews gathered secretly to study Torah. If an officer would discover them congregating, they would pretend to be gambling with a dreidel and thus escape arrest.

Playing the Dreidel Game

Any number of players can play dreidel. The dreidel is a four-sided top with the Hebrew letters _nun, gimel, hay,_ and _shin_ on it. These letters stand for _Nais Godol Hoyoh Shom_—"A Great Miracle Happened There." Each player puts a penny, candy, or nut into the "pot" and then, in turn, spins the top. The Hebrew character at which the dreidel stops determines the results. When it rests with _nun_ at the top, the player receives nothing from the pot. When the dreidel rests with _gimel_ at the top, the player receives all of the pot. If _hay_ is on the top, the player gets half of the pot. If _shin_ is on the top, the player puts back one item into the pot. The game is over when one player has managed to get the whole pot.

Balsa Wood Dreidel

Materials:
Balsa wood approximately 2" x 24"
Practice piece of balsa wood
Fine-toothed handsaw, hacksaw, or jigsaw
Marking pen
3" length of ¼" dowel

A balsa wood dreidel is a fun toy to use for the traditional Dreidel game. Cutting balsa wood is best done by an adult, but any child would enjoy helping out with the decorating and adding the dowel.

Draw cutting guidelines onto the balsa wood (illus. 3A). The dotted lines of the illustration represent your cutting lines. You want to carve a four-sided point onto the block. Test your saw on the practice piece of balsa wood. Practice cutting an angle.

Carve your block. Start at the dotted line that circles the block. Carve toward the dot on the top of the block. Your finished piece should resemble illustration 3B.

To prepare for the game-playing, sharpen a 3" length of dowel in a pencil sharpener and press it into the dreidel on the flat end. Use a marker pen to draw the Hebrew letters, as illustrated (illus. 3C).

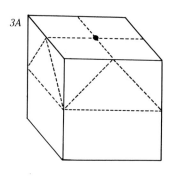

3A

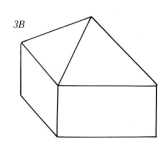

3B

3C ש

 ה

ג

נ

Shin   Hay   Gimel   Nun

Chanukah celebrations are especially fun for children—from lighting the candles to decorating the house and eating Mom's and Dad's homemade cookies.

From *Judas Maccabaeus*

ACT I
The Citadel of Antiochus at Jerusalem.

SCENE I—ANTIOCHUS; JASON.

Antiochus. O Antioch, my Antioch, my city!
Queen of the East! my solace, my delight!
The dowry of my sister Cleopatra
When she was wed to Ptolemy, and now
Won back and made more wonderful by me!
I love thee, and I long to be once more
Among the players and the dancing women
Within thy gates, and bathe in the Orontes,
Thy river and mine. O Jason, my High-Priest,
For I have made thee so, and thou art mine,
Hast thou seen Antioch the Beautiful?
Jason. Never, my Lord.
Ant. Then hast thou never seen
The wonder of the world. This city of David
Compared with Antioch is but a village,
And its inhabitants compared with Greeks
Are mannerless boors.
Jason. They are barbarians,
And mannerless.
Ant. They must be civilized.
They must be made to have more gods
than one;
And goddesses besides.
Jason. They shall have more.
Ant. They must have hippodromes, and games, and baths,
Stage-plays and festivals, and most of all
The Dionysia.
Jason. They shall have them all.
Ant. By Heracles! but I should like to see
These Hebrews crowned with ivy, and arrayed
In skins of fawns, with drums and flutes and thyrsi,
Revel and riot through the solemn streets
Of their old town. Ha, ha! It makes me merry
Only to think of it!—Thou dost not laugh.
Jason. Yea, I laugh inwardly.
Ant. The new Greek leaven
Works slowly in this Israelitish dough!
Have I not sacked the Temple, and on the altar
Set up the statue of Olympian Zeus
To Hellenize it?
Jason. Thou hast done all this.
Ant. As thou wast Joshua once and now art Jason,
And from a Hebrew hast become a Greek,
So shall this Hebrew nation be translated,
Their very natures and their names be changed,
And all be Hellenized.
Jason. It shall be done.
Ant. Their manners and their laws and way of living
Shall all be Greek. They shall unlearn their language,
And learn the lovely speech of Antioch.

SCENE III — ANTIOCHUS; JASON.

Ant. My task is easier than I dreamed.
These people
Meet me half-way. Jason, didst thou take note

How these Samaritans of Sichem said
They were not Jews? that they were Medes and Persians,
They were Sidonians, anything but Jews?
'T is of good augury. The rest will follow
Till the whole land is Hellenized.
Jason. My Lord,
These are Samaritans. The tribe of Judah
Is of a different temper, and the task
Will be more difficult.
Ant. Dost thou gainsay me?
Jason. I know the stubborn nature of the Jew.
Yesterday, Eleazer, an old man,
Being fourscore years and ten, chose rather death
By torture than to eat the flesh of swine.
Ant. The life is in the blood, and the whole nation
Shall bleed to death, or it shall change its faith!
Jason. Hundreds have fled already to the mountains
Of Ephraim, where Judas Maccabaeus
Hath raised the standard of revolt against thee.
Ant. I will burn down their city, and will make it
Waste as a wilderness. Its thoroughfares
Shall be but furrows in a field of ashes.
It shall be sown with salt as Sodom is!
This hundred and fifty-third Olympiad
Shall have a broad and blood-red seal upon it,
Stamped with the awful letters of my name,
Antiochus the God, Epiphanes!—

ACT III
The Battle-field of Beth-horon

SCENE II—JUDAS MACCABAEUS; JEWISH FUGITIVES.

Judas. Who and what are ye, that with furtive steps
Steal in among our tents?
Fugitives. O Maccabaeus,
Outcasts are we, and fugitives as thou art,
Jews of Jerusalem, that have escaped
From the polluted city, and from death.
Judas. None can escape from death. Say that ye come
To die for Israel, and ye are welcome.
What tidings bring ye?
Fugitives. Tidings of despair.
The Temple is laid waste; the precious vessels,
Censers of gold, vials and veils and crowns,
And golden ornaments, and hidden treasures,
Have all been taken from it, and the Gentiles
With revelling and with riot fill its courts,
And dally with harlots in the holy places.
Judas. All this I knew before.
Fugitives. Upon the altar
Are things profane, things by the law forbidden;
Nor can we keep our Sabbaths or our Feasts,
But on the festivals of Dionysus
Must walk in their processions, bearing ivy
To crown a drunken god.

Judas. This too I know.
But tell me of the Jews. How fare the Jews?
Fugitives. The coming of this mischief hath been sore
And grievous to the people. All the land
Is full of lamentation and of mourning.
The Princes and the Elders weep and wail;
The young men and the maidens are made feeble;
The beauty of the women hath been changed.
Judas. And are there none to die for Israel?
'T is not enough to mourn. Breastplate and harness
Are better things than sackcloth. Let the women
Lament for Israel; the men should die.
Fugitives. Both men and women die; old men and young:
Old Eleazer died: and Máhala
With all her Seven Sons.
Judas. Antiochus,
At every step thou takest there is left
A bloody footprint in the street, by which
The avenging wrath of God will track thee out!
It is enough. Go to the sutler's tents:
Those of you who are men, put on such armor
As ye may find; those of you who are women,
Buckle that armor on; and for a watchword
Whisper, or cry aloud, "The Help of God."

SCENE IV — JUDAS MACCABAEUS; CAPTAINS AND SOLDIERS.

Judas. The hour is come. Gather the host together
For battle. Lo, with trumpets and with songs
The army of Nicanor comes against us.
Go forth to meet them, praying in your hearts,
And fighting with your hands.
Captains. Look forth and see!
The morning sun is shining on their shields
Of gold and brass; the mountains glisten with them,
And shine like lamps. And we who are so few
And poorly armed, and ready to faint with fasting,
How shall we fight against the multitude?
Judas. The victory of a battle standeth not
In multitudes, but in the strength that cometh
From heaven above. The Lord forbid that I
Should do this thing, and flee away from them.
Nay, if our hour be come, then let us die;
Let us not stain our honor.
Captains. 'T is the Sabbath.
Wilt thou fight on the Sabbath, Maccabaeus?
Judas. Ay; when I fight the battles of the Lord,
I fight them on his day, as on all others.
Have ye forgotten certain fugitives
That fled once to these hills, and hid themselves
In caves? How their pursuers camped against them

Upon the Seventh Day, and challenged
them?
And how they answered not, nor cast a
stone,
Nor stopped the places where they lay
concealed,
But meekly perished with their wives and
children,
Even to the number of a thousand souls?
We who are fighting for our laws and lives
Will not so perish.
Captains. Lead us to the battle!
Judas. And let our watchword be, "The
Help of God!"

ACT IV
*The outer Courts of the
Temple of Jerusalem*

Scene I—Judas Maccabaeus; Captains; Jews.
Judas. Behold, our enemies are
discomfited.
Jerusalem is fallen; and our banners
Float from her battlements, and o'er her
gates
Nicanor's severed head, a sign of terror,
Blackens in wind and sun.
Captains. O Maccabaeus,
The citadel of Antiochus, wherein
The Mother with her Seven Sons was
murdered,
Is still defiant.
Judas. Wait.
Captains. Its hateful aspect
Insults us with the bitter memories
Of other days
Judas. Wait; it shall disappear
And vanish as a cloud. First let us cleanse
The Sanctuary. See, it is become
Waste like a wilderness. Its golden gates
Wrenched from their hinges and consumed
by fire;
Shrubs growing in its courts as in a forest;
Upon its altars hideous and strange idols;
And strewn about its pavement at my feet
Its Sacred Books, half burned and painted
o'er
With images of heathen gods.
Jews. Woe! woe!
Our beauty and our glory are laid waste!
The Gentiles have profaned our holy
places!

(Lamentation and alarm of trumpets.)

Judas. This sound of trumpets, and this
lamentation,
The heart-cry of a people toward the
heavens,
Stir me to wrath and vengeance. Go, my
captains;
I hold you back no longer. Batter down
The citadel of Antiochus, while here
We sweep away his altars and his gods.

ACT V
The Mountains of Ecbatana.

Scene I—Antiochus; Philip; Attendants.
Ant. Here let us rest awhile. Where are we,
Philip?
What place is this?
Philip. Ecbatana, my Lord;

And yonder mountain range is the Orontes.
Ant. The Orontes is my river at Antioch.
Why did I leave it? Why have I been
tempted
By coverings of gold and shields and
breastplates
To plunder Elymais, and be driven
From out its gates, as by a fiery blast
Out of a furnace?
Philip. These are fortune's changes.
Ant. What a defeat it was! The Persian
horsemen
Came like a mighty wind, the wind
Khamáseen,
And melted us away, and scattered us
As if we were dead leaves, or desert sand.
Philip. Be comforted, my Lord; for thou
hast lost
But what thou hadst not.
Ant. I, who made the Jews
Skip like the grasshoppers, am made myself
To skip among these stones.
Philip. Be not discouraged.
Thy realm of Syria remains to thee;
That is not lost nor marred.
Ant. O, where are now
The splendors of my court, my baths and
banquets?
Where are my players and my dancing
women?

Where are my sweet musicians with their
pipes,
That made me merry in the olden time?
I am a laughing-stock to man and brute.
The very camels, with their ugly faces,
Mock me and laugh at me.
Philip. Alas, my Lord,
It is not so. If thou wouldst sleep awhile,
All would be well.
Ant. Sleep from mine eyes is gone,
And my heart faileth me for very care.
Dost thou remember, Philip, the old fable
Told us when we were boys, in which the
bear
Going for honey overturns the hive,
And is stung blind by bees? I am that beast,
Stung by the Persian swarms of Elymais.
Philip. When thou art come again to
Antioch
These thoughts will be covered and
forgotten
As are the tracks of Pharaoh's chariot-
wheels
In the Egyptian sands.
Ant. Ah! when I come
Again to Antioch! When will that be?
Alas! alas!

Scene II — Antiochus; Philip; A Messenger.
Messenger. May the King live forever!

Ant. Who art thou, and whence comest
  thou?
Messenger. My Lord,
I am a messenger from Antioch,
Sent here by Lysias.
Ant. A strange foreboding
Of something evil overshadows me.
I am no reader of the Jewish Scriptures;
I know not Hebrew; but my High-Priest
  Jason,
As I remember, told me of a Prophet
Who saw a little cloud rise from the sea
Like a man's hand, and soon the heaven
  was black
With clouds and rain. Here, Philip, read; I
  cannot;
I see that cloud. It makes the letters dim
Before mine eyes.
Philip (reading). "To King Antiochus,
The God, Epiphanes."
Ant. O mockery!
Even Lysias laughs at me!—Go on, go on!
Philip (reading). "We pray thee hasten thy
  return. The realm
Is falling from thee. Since thou hast gone
  from us
The victories of Judas Maccabaeus
Form all our annals. First he overthrew
Thy forces at Beth-horon, and passed on,
And took Jerusalem, the Holy City.
And then Emmaus fell; and then Bethsura;
Ephron and all the towns of Galaad,
And Maccabaeus marched to Carnion."
Ant. Enough, enough! Go call my chariot-
  men;
We will drive forward, forward, without

ceasing,
Until we come to Antioch. My captains,
My Lysias, Gorgias, Seron, and Nicanor,
Are babes in battle, and this dreadful Jew
Will rob me of my kingdom and my crown.
My elephants shall trample him to dust;
I will wipe out his nation, and will make
Jerusalem a common burying-place,
And every home within its walls a tomb!
*(Throws up his hands, and sinks into the
  arms of attendants, who lay him upon
  a bank.)*
Philip. Antiochus! Antiochus! Alas,
The King is ill! What is it, O my Lord?
Ant. Nothing. A sudden and sharp spasm of
  pain,
As if the lightning struck me, or the knife
Of an assassin smote me to the heart.
'T is passed, even as it came. Let us set
  forward.
Philip. See that the chariots be in readiness;
We will depart forthwith.
Ant. A moment more.
I cannot stand. I am become at once
Weak as an infant. Ye will have to lead me.
Jove, or Jehovah, or whatever name
Thou wouldst be named,—it is alike to
  me,—
If I knew how to pray, I would entreat
To live a little longer.
Philip. O my Lord,
Thou shalt not die; we will not let thee die!
Ant. How canst thou help it, Philip? O the
  pain!
Stab after stab. Thou hast no shield against
This unseen weapon. God of Israel,

Since all the other gods abandon me,
Help me. I will release the Holy City,
Garnish with goodly gifts the Holy Temple.
Thy people, whom I judged to be unworthy
To be so much as buried, shall be equal
Unto the citizens of Antioch.
I will become a Jew, and will declare
Through all the world that is inhabited
The power of God!
Philip. He faints. It is like death.
Bring here the royal litter. We will bear him
Into the camp, while yet he lives.
Ant. O Philip,
Into what tribulation am I come!
Alas! I now remember all the evil
That I have done the Jews; and for this
  cause
These troubles are upon me, and behold
I perish through great grief in a strange
  land.
Philip. Antiochus! my King!
Ant. Nay, King no longer.
Take thou my royal robes, my signet-ring,
My crown and sceptre, and deliver them
Unto my son, Antiochus Eupator;
And unto the good Jews, my citizens,
In all my towns, say that their dying
  monarch
Wisheth them joy, prosperity, and health.
I who, puffed up with pride and arrogance,
Thought all the kingdoms of the earth mine
  own,
If I would but outstretch my hand and take
  them,
Meet face to face a greater potentate,
King Death—Epiphanes—the Illustrious!

—Henry Wadsworth Longfellow

The Feast of Lights

Kindle the taper like the steadfast star
  Ablaze on evening's forehead o'er the earth,
And add each night a luster till afar
  An eightfold splendor shine above thy hearth.
Clash, Israel, the cymbals, touch the lyre,
  Blow the brass trumpet and the harsh-tongued horn;
Chant psalms of victory till the heart takes fire,
  The Maccabean spirit leap newborn.

Remember how from wintry dawn till night,
  Such songs were sung in Zion, when again
On the high altar flamed the sacred light,
  And, purified from every Syrian stain,
The foam-white walls with golden shields were hung,
  With crowns and silken spoils, and at the shrine,
Stood, midst their conqueror-tribe, five chieftains sprung
  From one heroic stock, one seed divine.

Five branches grown from Mattathias's stem,
  The Blessed Johanan, the Keen-eyed Jonathan,
Simon the fair, the Burst-of-Spring, the Gem,
  Eleazar, Help-of-God; o'er all his clan
Judah the Lion-Prince, the Avenging Rod,
  Towered in warrior-beauty, uncrowned king,
Armed with the breastplate and the sword of God,
  Whose praise is: "He received the perishing."

They who had camped within the mountain pass,
  Couched on the rock, and tented 'neath the sky,
Who saw from Mizpeh's heights the tangled grass
  Choke the wide Temple courts, the altar lie
Disfigured and polluted—who had flung
  Their faces on the stones, and mourned aloud
And rent their garments, wailing with one tongue,
  Crushed as a windswept bed of reeds is bowed.

Even they by one voice fired, one heart of flame,
  Though broken reeds, had risen, and were men,
They rushed upon the spoiler and o'ercame,
  Each arm for freedom had the strength of ten.
Now is their mourning into dancing turned,
  Their sackcloth doffed for garments of delight,
Week-long the festive torches shall be burned,
  Music and revelry wed day with night.

Still ours the dance, the feast, the glorious psalm,
  The mystic lights of emblem, and the Word.
Where is our Judah? Where out five-branched palm?
  Where are the lion-warriors of the Lord?
Clash, Israel, the cymbals, touch the lyre,
  Sound the brass trumpet and the harsh-tongued horn,
Chant hymns of victory till the heart take fire,
  The Maccabean spirit leap newborn!

—Emma Lazarus

Mi Y'malël

Mi y'-ma-lël g'vu-rot Yis-ra-ël? O-tan mi yim-ne?

Hën b'-ḥol dor ya-kum ha-gi-bor go-ël ha-am.

Sh'ma!___ Ba-ya-mim ha-hëm ba-z'man ha-ze,___

Ma-ka-bi mo-shi-a u-fo-de,___

U-v'ya-më-nu kol am Yis-ra-ël,___

yit-a-ḥëd ya-kum l'-hi-ga-ël.

Latkes and Applesauce

Although there is no ritual food associated with Chanukah, dairy dishes have become a part of the holiday; to pay tribute to Judith, who saved her city by cleverly feeding wine and cheese to the enemy, we eat cheeses, sour cream, and cottage cheese. Potato latkes, so well known to Jewish families in the United States, are actually a corruption of Sephardic cheese latkes. European Jews did not have ready access to cheese, so they adapted the recipe to include an ingredient that they had in abundance—potatoes.

Many households still have a festive dinner on the fifth candle night of Chanukah. A goose, turkey, or chicken sits at center table, because the season marks the beginning of Passover preparations and the households must begin to reserve the fat from these birds. Some families, usually of Russian descent, celebrate with a Flaming Tea ceremony. Each guest and family member receives a lump of sugar and tongs, a pony of brandy and a glass of tea. First the sugar is dipped into the brandy, then a candle is passed around so that each celebrant may light his or her sugar before dropping it into the tea. Turn the lights out for proper atmosphere.

MENU
BREAKFAST AND SNACKS

◆

Potato Latkes

◆

Applesauce

◆

Mandel Bread

◆

Coin Cookies

Potato Latkes

6 medium potatoes
1 onion
2 eggs
2 tablespoons flour or matzo meal
1 teaspoon salt
Vegetable oil for frying

Pare and grate potatoes into a mixing bowl. Squeeze out liquid or drain in a colander for a few minutes. Peel and grate onion into the potatoes. Add the eggs and mix. Then add the flour and mix. Finally add the salt and stir to make a smooth batter that will drop heavily from the spoon.

Heat the oil in a frying pan, using enough to cover the latkes amply. Drop the batter from a tablespoon or other large spoon into the hot oil, making pancakes about 3 inches in diameter. (Note: Do not allow the oil to smoke, and remember to let the oil heat up again after every few latkes and after replenishing the oil.) Fry on the underside until brown; turn and brown the other side. Lift out and drain on paper towels.

Variation: Use the same batter but pour into a well-greased muffin pan and bake for 45 minutes in a preheated 350° F oven.

Applesauce

2 pounds apples
½ to 1 cup sugar
½ teaspoon lemon juice

Wash the apples, core, and cut into quarters. Cover with cold water and cook until soft, turning apples occasionally. When tender, put through a food mill or in a blender. Return the apples to the saucepan, add sugar to taste, and the lemon juice. Cook for 4 minutes over low heat. Pour into clean jars and store in the refrigerator.

Mandel Bread

3 eggs
Pinch salt
1 cup sugar
½ cup vegetable oil
1 teaspoon vanilla
1 teaspoon almond flavoring
2½ cups flour
3 teaspoons baking powder
1 cup sliced or slivered almonds (blanched)

Preheat the oven to 350° F.

Beat the eggs until very light. Add the salt and sugar and continue to beat. Add the oil gradually, beating well after each addition. Then add the vanilla and the almond flavoring. Mix well.

In a large mixing bowl, sift the flour with the baking powder; add the almonds and mix. Pour about a quarter of the dry-ingredient mixture into the egg mixture and combine until well blended. Repeat until the dry ingredients are mixed in thoroughly.

Grease and lightly flour cookie sheets or shallow baking pans and set aside. Turn the dough out and form long loaves about 2½-inches wide and 1-inch thick. Bake for 20 to 25 minutes. Remove and cut at an angle while still hot. Place on the baking sheet again and return to the oven to brown, for about 10 minutes.

Coin Cookies

2 cups sugar
1½ cups butter
4 eggs
4 cups sifted flour
4 teaspoons baking powder
1 teaspoon vanilla
6 ounces bittersweet chocolate
½ cup heavy cream

Cream the sugar and butter and mix well. In a small bowl, beat the eggs, then add to the sugar-butter mixture. Sift the flour with the baking powder and add. Then add the vanilla and mix well. Cover with waxed paper or plastic wrap and chill in the refrigerator overnight.

Preheat the oven to 400° F before you remove the cookie dough from the refrigerator. Roll the dough out and cut into ⅛-inch thick circles using a round cookie cutter or glass rim. Bake cookies for 10 to 12 minutes. Set aside to cool.

Chop the chocolate into chunks, then grind finely in a food processor. In a small saucepan, heat the cream until it just begins to simmer, remove from the heat, and with the food processor on, add to the chocolate in a stream. Blend until smooth. Set aside to cool and thicken. Do not stir. When both the cookies and the frosting are cool, spread the chocolate on the cookies.

Star-of-David Present

Materials:

One sheet of plastic needlepoint mesh with
⅛" holes
2 yards of light blue ⅛" wide ribbon
2 yards of light yellow ⅛" wide ribbon

This project has a geometric simplicity in
appearance, and just slightly more than that
in effort. The results are an elegant Chanukah symbol for a child to construct and give
to someone special. With adult assistance, a
child can tie on the ribbons and weave the
pattern quite easily.

Use illustration 3D as a guide and cut out
a piece of the plastic mesh into the shape of
the Star of David. It is important to actually
count off the individual squares, rather than
cutting at random. This is part of what
establishes your ribbon pattern. Your Star
will measure approximately 5" wide and
3½" tall.

Very carefully cut a slit into each square
around the perimeter of the star. By looking
at the photograph of the finished ornament,
you can see that these slits are the way that
you will lock each ribbon strand into the
needlepoint mesh. The squares hold the
ribbon in place as the pattern builds, and
they keep the ribbons evenly spaced. *Do not
cut the top corner mesh at "A".* This is
where you will tie on the hanging ribbon.

Since the needlepoint mesh comes in
sheets, usually 10" x 15" or so, you have
much additional mesh in the event that you
make a cutting error.

Begin by tying one of the ribbons onto
the corner mesh at A. Use about 6" of the
end to knot a loop which will be your
hanger. Then, without cutting the ribbon,
bring the ribbon around the front, as is
shown by the arrow, and sliding it through
the slit in the plastic square, bring it across
to point B.

At B, also slide the ribbon into the plastic
squares (by way of the slits), and bring the
ribbon *around* the point at B, as can be seen
in the photograph and through the path of
the arrows in illustration 3E. Bring the ribbon across the mesh to corner C, and repeat
the "wrapping." Once again you will have
slid the ribbon into the slits in order to form
the pattern.

Bring the ribbon up to A once again.

This time, use the next square on the left
side of the point and wrap around the point
at A again. You'll be bringing it around the
back and into the next square on the right
side of point A.

Repeat this pattern until you use up the
ribbon. Keep the rows smooth and the ribbons one next to the other. Tie the end at A
and tuck in the end behind the frame.

Tie the second ribbon onto the frame at
D. Bring the ribbon across the mesh to the

bottom of the Star at point E. Wrap around
the mesh at E in the same manner as you
did with your first ribbon. Then bring the
ribbon up to F and repeat. Continue to
make a wrapped triangle pattern of overlapping ribbons until you have used up the
second ribbon and have a triangle that
matches the first one, completing the Star-
of-David pattern. Tie on the ribbon end at D
and tuck the short end under the Star. Your
Star-of-David is ready for gift-giving!

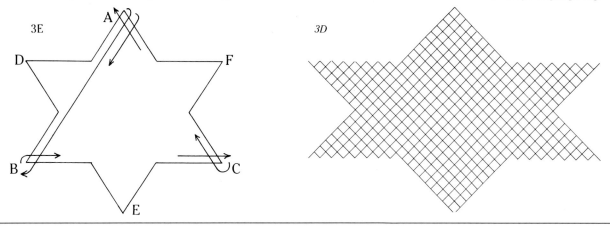

3E

3D

Chanukah Wall Hanging

Materials:
Scrap fabrics for menorah pieces and
*   flames*
¾ yard of background fabric for front &
*   back of wall hanging*
16 x 21" polyester craft batting
30" dowel (optional ¼" to ½" diameter)
24" gold cord

This project is constructed using machine-appliqued quilting techniques. Its finished size is 16" x 19½" from dowel to dowel.

Choosing the Fabrics
Any fabrics that complement the decor of your home would be appropriate for this cheerful Chanukah wall hanging. A choice of calico fabrics, or calico fabrics on a solid background, would coordinate well with a casual country-style room. In contrast, satins, laces, and polished cottons would achieve a more formal look. Take into account the wallpaper or painted wall in the room where the wall hanging will be displayed when you choose your fabrics.

Cutting Out the Pieces
Cut out a piece of craft batting 18" x 21". This batting will be sandwiched between the front and back layers of the wall hanging to create thickness and a soft texture.

Cut fabric pieces for front & back. Make one 18" x 27" (for front) and cut one 18" x 21" (for back). Cut out menorah pieces: eight pieces of A, one piece of B, nine pieces of C, one piece of D, and one piece of E (illus. 3I). A measures 1" x 3". B measures 2" x 5". C measures 1½" x ¾". D measures

6½" wide at the bottom and about 3½" tall. Use your imagination to cut out any style of menorah base. E measures 1 x 6½". Also cut out "Chanukah" from block letters, using the pattern provided. If desired you can create your own letters pattern.

Assembling the Wall Hanging
Place the two background pieces with *right sides together.* Center the smaller piece on top of the larger one so that 3" borders are at the top and bottom.

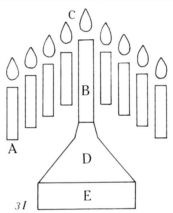

3I

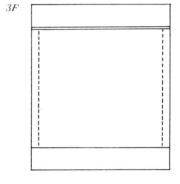

3F

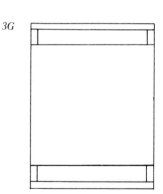

3G

3H

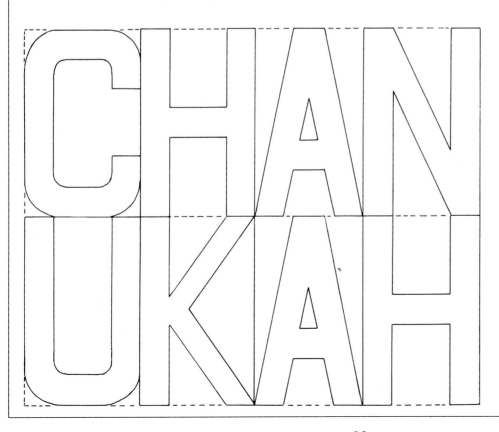

Place batting piece on top of the two layers. Pin along the 26″ edges. These will be the side seams of the hanging. Sew in straight stitch with ½″ seam allowance. (Illus. 3F) Trim batting to ¼″.

Turn right side out. You will have a prepared background with a batting sandwiched in between. The side seams will have created a finished edge along the sides.

To finish the top edges, turn in the side edges at the top and bottom, continuing along the ½″ seam. Iron. Then, turn in and iron a ½″ hem on the top and bottom of the front (the 26″ piece, as in illus. 3G). Fold down the top hem and machine stitch in place ½″ from the raw edge of the batting and back piece. A sleeve for the hanging dowel will be created. Using the sewing machine, edgestitch along the top fold. Repeat the folding, hemming, and edgestitching on the bottom of the wall hanging (illus. 3H).

Appliquéing Your Design
Now that your background is prepared, you are ready to position, pin, and appliqué your menorah pieces onto the background. Starting with the center piece B (the shamash), baste or carefully pin all of the menorah pieces and flame parts carefully onto the background. _Important: The hems of the main pieces should be on the back!_ Be sure that the layers of fabric and batting are perfectly even. When all of the pieces are pinned or basted in place, you may proceed to appliqué. Set your machine zigzag at a ¼″ wide plain zigzag.

It is very important that the stitching is begun in the _center_ of the wall hanging. Begin with the center piece B and zigzag around the piece, taking care to catch all of the raw edges and to keep your stitching lines straight. You will be stitching through the front, batting, and back fabrics as you attach each piece. Continue to zigzag appliqué each of the pieces onto the background, working from the center pieces first and sewing the pieces that are near the edge last.

Take care that the fabric layers remain smooth as you manipulate the fabric. The layers, combined with the appliquéd pieces, will create a slightly puffy, soft texture on the surface of the fabric.

You need not break the thread as you go from one piece to another. Simply lift the needle, move to the next piece, and continue. When all of the candle, flame, and base pieces have been stitched, just trim the thread ends that run from one piece to another on the front and the back.

Finishing Details
Cut the 36″ dowel in half, making two pieces 18″ long. Slide one into the top sleeve section and one into the bottom sleeve section. Tie the gold cord to each end of the top dowel. Your Chanukah wall hanging is ready to display and enjoy!

Children's Menorah

Materials:
Modeling clay which can be fired in a home oven
Birthday candles
Popsicle stick
Optional: Gloss finish

Constructing the Menorah
This project is an excellent Chanukah activity for parent and child to enjoy together.

Purchase modeling clay that is designed for firing (the process which hardens and sets the shape of the clay) in a home oven. The brand that we have used is an artist's clay type which bakes at 275° F. Most arts & crafts supply stores have some type of this clay available, although the firing temperature and preparation may vary. Be sure to adhere strictly to the directions on your package!

Using approximately 2″ chunks of clay, knead the pieces to make them extremely pliable. Children generally enjoy doing this part, long after you've become bored and eager to begin your creation. Don't begin shaping the clay until it is warm and soft. If you proceed without proper kneading, your menorah will have a rough-hewn look and it will be difficult to join the individual parts. Well-kneaded clay is also essential to forming intricate details on the surface—if this is what you have in mind.

Let your imagination be your guide as you and your assistants produce a group effort. Try to keep an open mind regarding the finished product. If your children are young, your menorah may look more primitive than our example, but please don't "fix up" their work too much! Nine to twelve year olds are the ones who are prone to roll out miles of tiny clay embellishments.

When the clay is ready to shape, roll out tiny snakes of clay about ¼″ in diameter and 2″ long. Use the popsicle stick as a base for the menorah. Use a birthday candle as a model for the size of the candle holders.

Coil the clay around the candle and then place the clay ring on the popsicle stick. The first ring should be placed in the center of the stick: it will be the shamash. This one should be more intricate than the other eight candle holders to set it apart.

Coil four candle holders for each side. Then, begin the creative part: Decorate and attach more details to the menorah. Different colors of clay may be rolled together for a marbelized effect. Or, they may be joined by simply pressing together. The more pliable your clay is, the easier it will be to embellish. A Star-of-David, scrolls, and decorative twists of clay will all add to the holiday appearance.

When you have finished your menorah, bake it in the oven to "fire" it, according to the manufacturer's instructions which came with your clay. Be sure that you do not bake it with any candles in it! After the menorah is thoroughly cooled, birthday candles may be inserted into the candle holders.

An optional finishing touch would be to glaze the hardened piece with the recommended glaze. Most clay manufacturers make a gloss or lacquer-type product to seal the clay and make it shiny.

Your children may enjoy making more than one of these to give as Chanukah gifts.

PURIM

The Festive Festival

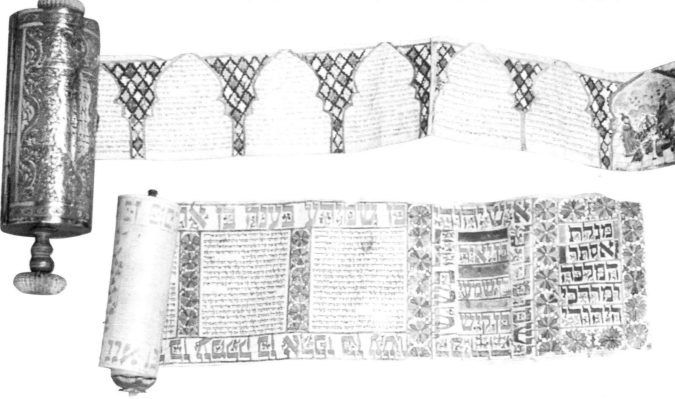

The festival of Purim, named after the *pur,* or "lots," Haman cast to determine the date of the Jews' destruction, occurs on the fourteenth day of Adar, the twelfth month of the Jewish calendar. Marked by an unusually festive atmosphere, Purim has become a favorite holiday for all—a day reserved for masquerades, carnivals, parades, and all manner of joyous revelry. Purim, according to the Midrash, is the only holiday that will continue in the world to come. What makes Purim unique— what grants the holiday a jubilant atmosphere unmatched by any other holiday?

The Month of Adar

Purim's festivity connects intimately with the month of Adar. The Talmud states: "With the advent of Adar, joy is increased." According to legend, the Jews attain a metaphysical power during Adar that protects them from their enemies. The source of Jewish strength during this month lies in the mystical connection of Adar with Torah and the constellation of fish. The sea nourishes and supports the fish just as the "sea" of Torah, traditionally associated with Adar, nourishes and supports the Jewish people. A Talmudic tale illuminates this analogy: The kingdom ruling Israel adopted a decree banning the study of Torah. Papus the son of Judah, upon discovering Rabbi Akiva in defiance of the decree, inquired if the Rabbi were not afraid. Rabbi Akiva answered with an analogy. A fox was walking along the river bank and saw a school of fish moving to and fro. The fox asked the fish why they were scurrying about,

and the fish replied that they feared the fishermen's nets. The fox, wanting to help, invited them to come ashore where he would protect them. The fish, calling the fox a fool, answered that if they were afraid in water—the medium in which they live—they would certainly be afraid on land, where they would surely die. Rabbi Akiva continued and said that the same situation exists with the Jew. The Jew needs the Torah to live and thus cannot abstain even if the government bans Torah study. The mystical relationship between Adar and Torah study grants the month a special status, making it altogether appropriate that Purim occurs during Adar.

Megillat Esther

The story of Purim is recounted in the Megillah (the scroll of the story of Esther). It is read twice on the holiday—once at night and once during the day. All aspects of the holiday flow from the Megillah, so for a full understanding of Purim, one must be thoroughly familiar with the tale.

In the third year of his reign, King Ahashverosh (also known as Ahasuerus and Ahashuerus), wanting to display his great wealth and to solidify his power, decided to have a feast. Simultaneously, Queen Vashti initiated a celebration for the women of the realm. On the seventh day of festivities, the King, having had much to drink,

Haman pleads for Esther's forgiveness while King Ahashverosh looks on **right.**

summoned Vashti and ordered her to appear and demonstrate her beauty for the King's officials. Vashti refused to appear. (According to the Talmud, God afflicted her with leprosy to cause her downfall and Esther's rise.) Incensed, the King sought the advice of his officers as to a suitable punishment. One advisor, Memuchan, who according to at least one rabbi was actually Haman, argued that Vashti should be killed for her disobedience. The King followed his advice.

Some time passed and the King remembered Vashti and regretted his action. Desiring a new queen, the King, following his servant's advice, initiated a contest among all the eligible girls in his kingdom. One of those brought to Shushan, the capital, was Esther, a Jewish girl raised by her relative Mordechai after her parents' death. Mordechai instructed Esther not to divulge her Jewishness, and he kept in close contact with her; each day he walked by the court and inquired as to her well-being. Esther impressed all who met her, including the King, and she was elevated to queen in Vashti's place.

After a number of years, the King elevated Haman, a descendant of Amalek, the traditional enemy of the Jews, to a position above all other officials. Haman commanded respect and all bowed down to him except Mordechai, who refused to bow because, according to the Midrash, Haman wore an idol around his neck. Not content to punish Mordechai, Haman wanted to destroy the entire Jewish people, and he cast lots to determine the day of annihilation. Haman went to the King, slandered the Jews, and received permission to do as he wished. Upon learning of the plot, Mordechai tore his clothes, wore sackcloth and ashes, and entered the city crying loudly. Upon being told of Mordechai's display, Esther immediately dispatched a messenger to discover what was troubling her relative. Mordechai recounted the details of the evil decree and instructed Esther to intercede on the Jews' behalf. Esther replied that one who appears before the King unsummoned incurs the death penalty, unless the King extends his golden scepter. Mordechai repeated his request, stating that perhaps Esther was appointed queen for this purpose and that if she would not intercede even her royal status would not

protect her from the evil decree. Esther agreed to appear before the King and instructed Mordechai to organize a three-day fast for all the Jews on her behalf.

After completing the three-day fast, Esther entered the King's inner court clothed in her most royal garb. Upon seeing her, the King extended his golden scepter and inquired as to Esther's desires. Esther replied that she wished to invite the King and Haman to a banquet. At the feast, Esther repeated the invitation for the next night. Haman left the banquet consumed with self-importance and pride, but these feelings were transformed into anger when he saw Mordechai. Haman went home, and his wife, Zeresh, advised him to construct a gallows fifty cubits high upon which to hang Mordechai. Haman joyously acted upon the suggestion.

That night, the King could not sleep. Consequently, he ordered his servants to read from the book of chronicles, whereupon Ahashverosh discovered that Mordechai had never been rewarded for saving him from the assassination plot of two servants. Suddenly, Haman appeared in the court, and the King decided that his trusted servant should determine Mordechai's compensation. Haman, intending to obtain the King's permission to hang Mordechai, unwittingly answered the King's questions. The King asked Haman, "What should be done for the man the King wishes to reward?" Haman, believing that Ahashverosh intended to reward *him*, replied that the honoree should be dressed in royal clothing, ride upon a royal horse, and be led through the city streets by a government official proclaiming, "This

is what is done to the man the King wishes to honor." Ahashverosh agreed and instructed Haman to carry it out for Mordechai. Crestfallen, Haman followed the King's orders. Heaping insult upon insult, Haman's daughter, mistakenly believing that her father was being led by Mordechai, dumped garbage on her father, the horse's leader. Immediately after this episode, Haman was whisked away to Esther's second banquet where his downfall continued. Speaking poetically, Esther asked the King to "grant me my soul and my people," and she revealed Haman's villainous plot. Consumed with anger, Ahashverosh ordered that Haman be hanged on the gallows intended for Mordechai. Thereupon, the King elevated Mordechai to a position of great influence and allowed him to issue edicts permitting the Jews to fight their enemies. On the thirteenth of Adar, as well as on the fourteenth in Shushan, the Jews won tremendous victories and were saved from the threat of total annihilation.

The laws and customs of Purim all stem from this story of the triumph of good over evil. God, although not mentioned even once in the Megillah, is understood to have controlled and manipulated all the action. Perhaps this aspect of the holiday, the hidden hand of God, grants Purim its power, importance, and even its festivity. There exists no moment of obvious divine intervention, but the grandeur of God's design becomes apparent when one considers the entire tale.

A scribe writes a Megillah, **left.** *Prune hamantashen,* **below,** *are eaten during Purim.*

Ta'anit Esther

The fast of Esther, occurring on the thirteenth day of Adar, commemorates the Jews' fast during the Purim episode. The Jews battled their enemies on the thirteenth and they fasted on that day to ask for God's help in vanquishing the foe. Fasting demonstrates the Jewish belief that God's mercy brings victory; military prowess alone would be insignificant without God's help.

The Fourteenth or the Fifteenth?

While most cities around the world celebrate Purim on the fourteenth of Adar, certain cities celebrate the holiday on the fifteenth. This discrepancy originated during the time of Mordechai and Esther. In most of Ahashverosh's kingdom, the Jews fought their enemies on the thirteenth and rested from their battles on the fourteenth, marking the fourteenth as a day of celebration. In Shushan, though, the Jews fought on the thirteenth and fourteenth and didn't rest until the fifteenth. By rights, therefore, Purim the world-over should be on the fourteenth, while in Shushan alone it should be on the fifteenth. The rabbis, however, seeking to remember the land of Israel in this miracle, decreed that Shushan and all cities that were surrounded by a wall at the time of Joshua (which includes Jerusalem) should celebrate Purim on the fifteenth, while all other cities keep Purim on the fourteenth.

The Laws of Purim

In addition to reading the Megillah, there are three other commandments that must be performed on Purim: giving gifts to the poor, sending food packages, and eating a festive meal.

All Jews are commanded to give gifts to the poor, *matanot laevyonim,* during the day of Purim. One must give at least two gifts—of money, food, or clothes—to two indigents. The lone proviso calls for the gift to be important and significant. One must also give a gift of food, *mishloach manot,* to a friend—at least two types of ready-to-eat food to one person.

The commandments of matanot laevyonim and mishloach manot promote unity and friendship among Jews, and the connection of this laudable goal to Purim is obvious. The Jews fasted together to promote Esther's well-being and they fought together for their own survival. The enemies of the Jews can be victorious only if the Jews are separate and divided; if unified, the Jews can't be destroyed. One eats the festive meal, or *Seudat Purim,* on the fourteenth of Adar in the afternoon; it should consist of meat and wine. The presence of wine at the meal commemorates the fact that wine was integral to the Purim story. Ahashverosh killed Vashti because he was drunk, enabling Esther to assume the throne. The Talmud states that one must drink until he cannot differentiate between "cursed is Haman" and "blessed is Mordechai." Only on Purim does such a dictum exist, and the idea that the rabbis would command

someone to drink excessively requires explanation. To understand the principle behind this strange Talmudic statement, one must recall that the miracle of Purim, although seemingly lacking in divine intervention, actually represents the ultimate expression of God's protection of the Children of Israel. To demonstrate this, the Jew places himself completely in God's hands by drinking enough to attain a level of complete confusion. Such an interpretation fits well with the other often-cited explanation, that one should simply drink enough to get drowsy and go to sleep. When sleeping one demonstrates the belief that God will protect him and will "return" his soul in the morning. Thus, this strange custom actually represents a belief in Divine Providence.

The wearing of costumes may be the most entertaining of the Purim customs. Children particularly enjoy dressing as Ahashverosh, Vashti, Esther, Mordechai, and even Haman, clothing themselves to hide their true identity. As with most rituals, this one expresses a deep, fundamental truth about the holiday; it is not simple frivolity. God's presence was not obvious during the events. Purim is a hidden miracle; mistaken identity plays an important role in the holiday. This may originate in Esther's concealment of her Jewish heritage or Haman's mistaken belief that the King wished to reward him. It also appears in the dictum that we drink until we can't distinguish between Haman and Mordechai. In any event, the costumes add to the extreme festivity of the Purim atmosphere.

Purim is a great holiday for children, who can make costumes for themselves, deliver mishloach manot in baskets, and participate in community parades, carnivals, and games.

Hag Purim

Hag pu - rim, hag pu - rim, hag ga - dol hu la - u'hu - dim,

ma - së - hot, ra'a - sha - nim, z'mi - rot, ri - ku - dim.

CHORUS:

Ha - va nar - i - sha, rash, rash, rash, Ha - va nar - i - sha, rash, rash, rash,

Ha - va nar - i - sha, rash, rash, rash, ba - ra - a - sha - nim.

II. Hag pu-rim, hag pu-rim,
   ze el ze shol-him ma-not.
   Mah-ma-dim, mam-ta-kim,
   Tu-fi-nim, mig-da–not
chorus

The Banquet of Esther

While copious flowed the banquet wine,
    The king addressed his lovely queen.
"But ask, and all thou wilt I'll give."
        'Her tears now supplicate him.'

"O king, my lord, I humbly crave
    My life, and more my people's life.
For we are sold a bitter foe
        'Since thou didst yield before him.'

"What other wish could now be mine,
    With violence so rank afoot?
Could I betray my kin to fangs
        'Of beast that would devour him?' "

The king cried out: 'What subject this,
    Or who in all my broad domain,
Or who among my creditors
        'Dare ween you're sold to please him?' "

She spake, "This Haman fell, malign,
    Who voids his venom on my folk."
O woe unto the evil man;
        'His plotting shall undo him.'

The king in wrath his garden paced;
    Returned, sees Haman abject, vile.
The very skies revealed his guilt,
        'And earth rose up against him.'

A faithful chamberlain said, "See
    His gallows made for Mordecai."
The king cried out, "Hang Haman high!
        'The gallows loomed before him.' "

Queen Esther urged her people's plight;
    The edict dire must be annulled.
For how could one smite Israel!
        'Unless God planned to heal him?'

Forthwith an edict was prepared
    To arm the Jews against their foes.
Good Mordecai in power grew;
        'The peace of God possessed him.

His people breathed fair freedom's air
    When he was made Chief Minister
With honors great, in Haman's place
        'Of power to succeed him.'

Then Persia's Jews in self defence
    Rose up to guard themselves from hurt.
Through Haman's machinations foul
        'His sons met death beside him,'

Parshandatha, Dalfon, Aspatha,
    Poratha, Adalia, Aridatha,
Parmashta, Arisai, Aridai, Vaizatha.
        'The earth would not receive him.'

Delivered from the yawning grave,
    The Jews hurled back each fell assault.
God's succor strong upheld the weak
        'And poor with none to aid him.'

Be this now writ indelibly
    That age to age may ne'er forget,
And he who reads may sing, "Let man
        'Rejoice when God protects him.' "

So feast, good friends, go eat and drink;
    Purim shall be your merry feast.
But in your joy seek out the poor
        'With gifts; do not forget him.'

From ancient time God's providence
    Has borne me o'er engulfing tides.
For this my spirit counsels me,
        'Thy hope is God; await Him.'

—YEHUDAH HALEVI
Translated by David de Sola Pool

Purim

Come, quaff the brimming festal glass!
    Bring forth the good old cheer!
For Esther's Feast has come at last—
    Most gladsome in the year.

And now, when hearts beat glad and free,
    Come gather all about,
And tell once more how, long since, He
    Did put our foe to rout.

Full oft has beauty ruled a land,
    And held its sceptred sway;
Full often foiled th' avenging hand
    And bade oppression stay.

But ne'er did beauty so avail
    As when fair Esther's charm
'Gainst vengeful Haman did prevail
    To 'fend the Jews from harm.

So all the dire impending woe
    That hovered o'er their head
Did light upon their ruthless foe
    And ruined him, instead.

And thus, throughout the ages long,
    In every land and clime,
They chant an old thanksgiving song
    E'er mindful of that time.

Yea, Israel's Guardian never sleeps—
    No slumber to His eye!—
But loving watch He ever keeps
    Upon His flock from high.

—C. DAVID MATT

The Judgments of Reb Yozifel

Based on the story of Sholem Aleichem
Adapted by Solomon Schneider

In Kasrielevky, mishloach manot marked a time when the inhabitants of the good households of the town sent plates of hamentashen, cakes, cookies, and other sweets to neighbors, friends, and the poor folk. All through the day children and servants scurried through the streets, delivering and returning with plates of delectable delights, often receiving a small tip for the service.

Of course, mishloach manot was not solely a religious act or even a philanthropic custom. It had developed into a precise social ritual. There were gradations and precedents. For although a disparity in gifts was expected in exchanges between the poor and the well-to-do, God help you if you sent more than you received to someone who was considered of inferior status, or less than you received if your own inferiority was not established.

How seriously the code was taken, and what might occur if it were ignored or contravened, can be seen from the story of the two Nehamas. Nehama the black worked for Zlote, the wife of Isaac the storekeeper, and Nehama the red worked for Zelda, the wife of Yossie the storekeeper. One Purim the two Nehamas came face to face as they carried their trays to each other's employers. Tired of delivering gifts all over town, they sat down on the doorstep to swap stories, compare tips and revile their employers.

They also showed each other the contents of their trays. Nehama the black carried a square of strudel, two honey cakes, a poppyseed cake, and a honeyed-nut confection. Nehama the red carried a rich hamentash, two sponge cakes, a large golden cookie, and a thin-crusted cake filled with honey-laced nuts and raisins topped with sugar. The gifts were carefully balanced in terms of the relative status of the senders.

Tired and hungry, as well as feeling a touch rebellious, the Nehamas wondered if any harm would befall them if they were to remove an equal amount of cakes from each tray. If a honey cake disappeared from Zlote's plate and a sponge cake were taken from Zelda's would they not remain balanced? If the nut-filled cake and the honeyed nuts were removed would any harm be done? And was it not appropriate that the food feed the servant girls and not the vanity of their employers? As soon as it was plotted, it was done. But the servant girls neglected two crucial facts: Zelda and Zlote would undoubtedly remember what they had sent but would see only what they received in return, and each would be slighted by the diminished plates which did not take into account the status of the receivers. And of course each was slighted. When Nehama the red arrived at Zlote's abode with her lightened load she was yelled at and kicked out, while Nehama the black's delivery almost caused Zelda to faint.

It would have been bad enough had the two couples merely known each other. But the wives were friends who shared pots and gossip, and the husbands' stores were adjacent to each other in the market area. So the next day, after Isaac and Yossie came to open their shops, each stood outside by their respective doors, hoping the other would say "Good morning" so that he could snub him. But both stood there until their wives arrived.

"Isaac," said Zlote acidly, "did you thank your friend for his wonderful mishloach manot?"

"Yossie," said Zelda, "why don't you thank your good friend for his generous gift?"

With "I don't speak to that no good cheapskate" from each storekeeper, the battle began. Instantaneously, the husbands were at each other's throats and the wives in each other's hair. Half of the town quickly assembled to separate the combatants, join the melee, or simply observe. Before day's end, the feuding couples and their partisans invaded the home of Reb Yozifel, the old and beloved rabbi of Kasrielevky.

Reb Yozifel sat for several hours as accusations and counter-accusations flew across his living room. Finally the couples quieted down and demanded that Reb Yozifel act as judge.

Before the judgment Reb Yozifel, in his weak voice, began thus: "We are approaching Passover, the great festival, the festival that is without an equal in the Jewish calendar. Because of the freedom gained during this holiday, we received the holy Torah. And what is written in the gift God gave us? *Va'ahavta l'reakha kamokha*—love thy neighbor as thyself. Shall we in this way honor our neighbors and our Torah—with quarrels and silly disputes? We should concern ourselves with preparations for Passover, bake matzot, make sure there are enough eggs, potatoes, and wine. And we must make sure that the poor have enough to eat also. Do you realize how much work this entails? Should we spend precious time squabbling?"

Thus continued Reb Yozifel in his sad voice, until one by one the spectators withdrew, followed by the litigants, each going home embarrassed, wondering what the excitement had been all about, and now ready to prepare for Passover.

Could King Solomon have done better?

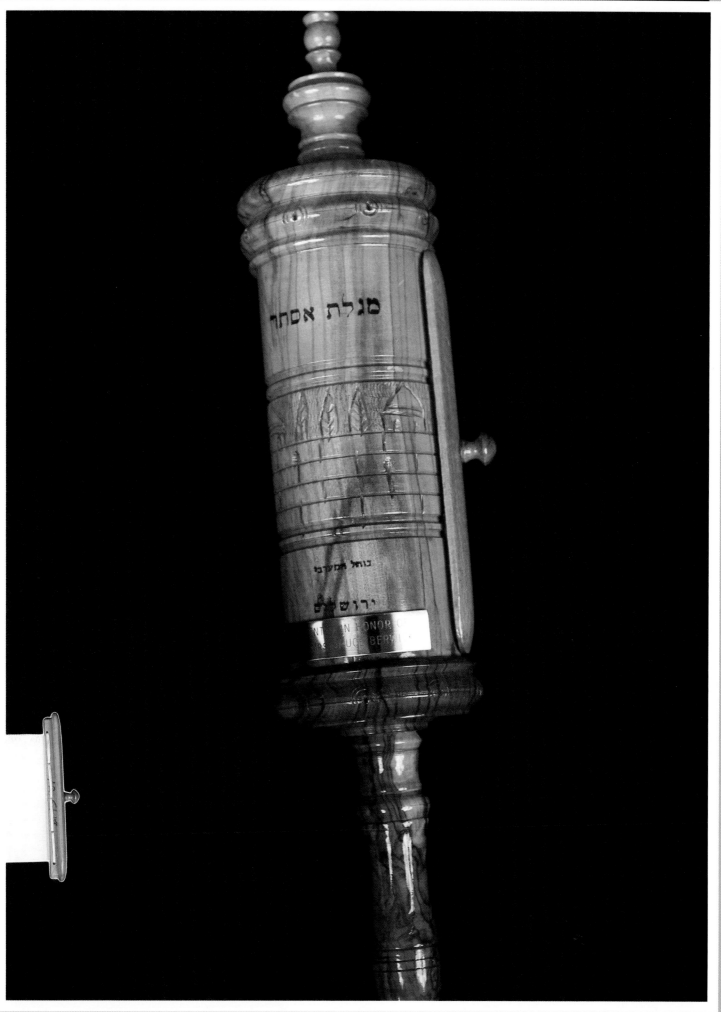

Hamantashen and Other Treats

One of the nicest traditions on Purim is _matanot laev-yonim,_ the giving of gifts to the poor. The tradition also includes a command to give gifts of food to friends, _mishloach manot._ With these two laws, Purim marks a time of heavenly smells emanating from the kitchen, children taking part in the cooking, and sweets galore.

Poppy seeds appear in many foods during Purim. The German word _mohn_ sounds like ha-_man,_ and so poppy seeds are cooked and eaten, making Haman helpless. The pastry also represents the three-cornered hat Haman wore.

Children can take part by stuffing dates and rolling them in sugar or they can cut out gingerbread Hamans and decorate them with raisins. Older kids can pinch the hamantashen or slice the poppy seed cookies.

MENU
FOODS TO GIVE
◆
Stuffed Dates
◆
Prune Hamantashen
◆
Meringues Plus
◆
Poppy Seed Cookies
◆
Drunken Pound Cake
◆
Fruit Compote

Stuffed Dates

24 dates

24 whole walnuts or other nutmeats

½ cup granulated sugar

Pit the dates if necessary. Press a nut into each date. To coat the dates, either roll them in a bowl of sugar or toss them in a paper bag that is filled with sugar.

Variation: Use prunes instead of the dates.

Hamantashen

Filling

1 pound pitted prunes, stewed

1 cup nutmeats

¼ teaspoon orange zest

½ teaspoon cinnamon

1 tablespoon sugar

1 tablespoon lemon juice

Chop the prunes and the nutmeats. Add the orange zest and the cinnamon and mix. Add the sugar, then taste. If more sugar is desired,

add another 1 to 3 teaspoons. Add the lemon juice and combine thoroughly. Set aside.

Dough

¼ pound butter

1 cup sugar

3 egg yolks

½ pint sour cream

3 cups flour

2 teaspoons baking powder

¼ teaspoon baking soda

1 teaspoon vanilla

⅛ teaspoon orange zest

Cream butter and sugar together until well mixed. In a separate bowl, beat the egg yolks. Add the beaten egg yolks to the butter-sugar mixture, then add the sour cream.

In a large mixing bowl, sift together the flour, baking powder, and baking soda; add the dry ingredients to the butter-sugar mixture. Then add the vanilla and orange zest. Mix well. Cover securely with wax paper or plastic wrap. Let stand in the refrigerator overnight.

Preheat oven to 350°F.

Roll out ¼-inch thick and cut into 3½-inch rounds. Stir the filling and place a heaping teaspoon into the center of each round. Draw up two sides of the dough and then the third, pinching the edges in the center of the round to form a three-cornered "pocket" for the filling. Place on a greased baking sheet and bake for about 20 minutes or until lightly browned.

Meringues Plus

2 egg whites

⅛ teaspoon salt

⅛ teaspoon cream of tartar

1 teaspoon vanilla

¾ cup sugar

¼ cup chopped nuts or raisins

1 6-ounce package of chocolate bits

Preheat oven to 300°F.

Beat egg whites with salt, cream of tartar, and vanilla until soft peaks form. Add sugar slowly and beat until stiff peaks form. Fold in nuts and chocolate. Grease cookie sheet and dust lightly with flour. Drop by heaping teaspoonful on sheet and bake for 25 minutes.

Poppy Seed Cookies

1 cup unsalted butter
¾ cups sugar
2 eggs
⅜ cup poppy seed
1½ teaspoon vanilla
2½ cups flour
1½ teaspoon baking powder
¼ teaspoon salt

Cream the butter with the sugar; add the eggs, poppy seed, and vanilla and mix well. Sift the dry ingredients and add to the poppy seed mixture. The dough will be a little sticky. Mix into a ball. Divide into rolls about 10 inches long; the cookies can be oval-shaped or round, about 2 inches in diameter. Roll the dough into floured wax paper or greased and floured parchment paper. Refrigerate overnight.

Preheat the oven to 375°F.

Slice thinly and bake on a greased cookie sheet for 10 to 12 minutes.

Variation: Add just enough flour to make the dough easy to roll. Cut with cookie cutters and brush a beaten egg yolk on the top of the cookie before baking for a glazed effect.

Drunken Pound Cake

3½ cups all-purpose flour, sifted
2 teaspoons baking powder
1½ cups butter, softened
2½ cups light brown sugar
½ cup dark brown sugar
1 tablespoon vanilla
½ teaspoon ginger
½ teaspoon cloves
½ teaspoon salt
5 large eggs
½ cup bourbon
½ cup milk or half and half
Cornmeal or breadcrumbs

Sift flour and baking powder together and set aside. Butter a 10-inch by 4-inch tube pan and line the bottom with wax paper. Butter the paper and dust the pan with fine cornmeal or breadcrumbs.

In a clean bowl, cream butter and sugar until light and fluffy. Add vanilla, ginger, cloves, and salt; then add the eggs, one at a time, beating well after each addition. Add sifted dry ingredients gradually, alternating with blended bourbon and milk. When all ingredients are well incorporated, pour the batter into the prepared tube pan, tapping the pan gently to make sure that the batter is level.

Bake at 350° for 1 hour and 20 minutes or until the cake is springy to the touch and a toothpick comes out dry. Cool for 15 minutes before inverting, putting on a plate, and glazing. Let the pound cake sit overnight before slicing. It will last for a week or so if tightly sealed to prevent drying.

Glaze

⅓ cup granulated sugar
⅓ cup bourbon
Juice of one lemon

Dissolve sugar, bourbon, and lemon juice in a small saucepan over low heat. Baste the cake with the glaze while both are still warm.

Fruit Compote

½ cup raisins, regular or golden
12 dried, pitted prunes
20 dried apricots
1 lemon
1 orange
6 strips lemon zest
6 strips orange zest
2 tart apples
2 bosc pears
1 quart sweet white wine
1 cup sugar
4 tablespoons honey
2 whole cloves
Pinch of ginger
1 cinnamon stick

Plump the raisins, prunes, and apricots by soaking in water for 2 hours. Drain. Cut the strips of orange and lemon zest, then peel the lemon and orange, removing as much white as possible, and slice thinly. Core the pears and apples and cut them into thick slices. Combine the wine, sugar, honey, zests, cloves, ginger, and cinnamon.

Bring the wine mixture to a simmer in a saucepan, then add the orange and lemon slices and the pears; poach for approximately 20 minutes, or until the pears are tender. Remove the citrus slices and the pears and place in a large bowl. Add the apple to the wine mixture and poach until tender, about 7 minutes. Remove and add to the pears and

citrus. Add the raisins, prunes, and apricots to the simmering liquid and poach until tender, about 15 or 20 minutes. Remove and add to the bowl of fruit. Pour syrup over the fruit to your liking.

Variation: Substitute fresh peaches, plums, and cherries for the dried fruit. Poach until tender, about 10 minutes.

King and Queen Costumes

Materials:

Approximately ½ yard of white or gold felt
for tiara and crown parts
Assorted colors of felt scraps for "jewels"
Plastic headband for tiara
White glue in squeeze bottle
Glitter and sequins to decorate costume
parts
1 yard gold cord
Cardboard strip to use as base for crown
Stapler

Assembling and Decorating the Tiara

First, prepare a paper pattern for the main part of the tiara: It should be a rectangle 10″ x 7″. Cut felt to size. Next, fold felt in half lengthwise and cut out a pointed-edged tiara shape, as shown in illustration.

Cut out "jewels" from felt scraps, making them assorted sizes and colors. Protect your work surface with a sheet of newspaper. Squeeze a line of glue along one side of the tiara, two inches from the centerfold, as shown in illus. 4A. Next, carefully place the felt tiara around the headband, as illustrated in 4B, pressing the glued side to its matching opposite side. Let dry for a few minutes. You may staple the points for extra reinforcement.

Apply dots of glue wherever you would like to attach the assorted colors and shapes of felt "jewels." Press "jewels" into place. Likewise, apply dots of glue to mark the position of the sequins, and then, press the sequins into place. You should, of course, use your imagination, and decorate either front or both the front and back of the tiara.

Finally, use the glue to "draw" designs for the glitter. Do one side first. Sprinkle the glitter onto the glue designs. Shake off excess. Repeat with the second side.

Tiara

4A

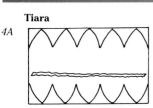
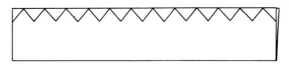

Crown

4B

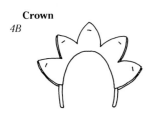
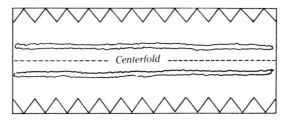

Centerfold

Don't attempt to try on the tiara until the glue is completely dry (and clear in color). While this part dries, proceed to create your next part of the costume!

Assembling and Decorating the Crown

To determine the size of the crown, measure circumference of head. Use this measurement *plus one inch* to prepare pattern pieces according to the illustration.

Next, lay out main piece of crown according to cutting directions. Be sure to place the pattern on the fold in order to have a double thickness crown—a more stable and secure design. Cut out "jewels" from the scraps, making them assorted colors and shapes.

Cut a strip of cardboard, making its measurement the circumference of the head *plus 3 inches*. This will provide enough overlap to account for any discrepancies in your original measurement. Use a stapler to fasten the two ends of the cardboard together with the ends overlapping 3 inches. Then, using the glue bottle, apply a line of glue to the crown felt, drawing it ½" away from the centerfold. Draw a second line of glue on the opposite side of the centerfold, as illustrated. Fold the crown around the cardboard circle. The cardboard will act as a form and will help the crown hold its shape, especially as the glue dries and stiffens. You have cut the crown felt 1" larger than the circumference measurement, so you'll be able to overlap the edges about 1". For additional strength, staple these overlapping edges. Let the crown dry for a few minutes.

Now, you are ready to decorate. Apply dots of glue wherever you would like "jewels." Press the felt scrap "jewels" onto the crown. Then, apply dots of glue wherever you would like sequins. Press the sequins in place.

Finally, "draw" with the glue bottle to make designs for the glitter. Sprinkle the glitter onto the wet glue, shake off the residue and let dry. Your crown is ready to wear!

Assembling and Decorating a "Jeweled" Neckpiece

To create a jeweled neckpiece, use the gold cord as the necklace base and fastener. Cut rectangles (approximately 1" x 4") and diamond shapes (5" long and about 2" wide). Apply glue to one half of each shape and fold over the cord, arranging them as desired. The photograph will give you some ideas.

Finally, embellish your "jeweled" neckpiece with felt scrap cut-outs, sequins, and glitter to match your tiara and crown. Tie the gold cord, adjusting the length so that it may be put over your head without untying it every time!

These costume accessories may be worn with anything from a simple t-shirt to a pretty party dress.

Noisemaker Toys (Graggers)

Materials:

Juice cans (rinsed and dried)
Contac® paper or other adhesive-backed paper
Stickers and/or colored tape for decorating
Jingle bells
Scissors
Glitter
White glue
Floral wire or pipecleaners

Graggers are an essential part of a child's celebration of Purim. Each time Haman's name is read, the children rattle their noisemakers to exorcise the enemy. Noisemakers are a fun and easy project which can be made, with adult assistance, by preschool age children and up. To prepare the juice can for decoration, trace the circular end onto the Contac® paper. Draw another circle 1" away from the outline circle, as illustrated. Cut out along the outside edge. With scissors, make cuts spaced 1" apart around the circle, from the outside to the inside. Make two of these adhesive paper circles, one for each end of the juice can.

Peel off the backing. Use this ring to cover the *closed* end of the juice can, as shown. Place 1 or 2 jingle bells inside. An adult can poke a hole in the center of the closed metal or plastic end of the can. Bend the floral wire or pipe cleaner in half and insert the two ends into the hole. On the inside, twist the two ends of the wire to prevent them from slipping back through the can. The wire loop on the outside of the can will be your handle.

Attach a second paper circle over the *open* end of the can, sealing the jingle bells inside.

Next, cut a strip of adhesive paper which is the width of the can and is long enough to wrap around the can with 1" of overlap. Carefully remove paper backing and wrap around the can. This strip will cover the entire outside of the juice can. Your noisemaker now is capable of making noise—but let's decorate it.

You can use any kind of colored tape to make stripes or decorative shapes and symbols. Or, choose some of your favorite stickers and use them to make a design on the noisemaker! Lastly, draw decorative lines with white glue and sprinkle them with glitter. Shake off the excess and listen to the gragger!

PASSOVER

A Celebration of Liberation

Pesach, the Passover holiday, begins on the fifteenth night of Nissan. On that night, during the festive meal called the *seder*, the youngest child of the family asks, "Why is this night different from all other nights?"

The Story of Exodus

According to tradition, the Jewish people were enslaved by the Egyptian empire under the rule of Ramses II, three thousand years ago. Their servitude, both bitter and oppressive, saw no hope of manumission. The story told in the second book of the Pentateuch, Exodus, relates how God instructed Moses, a Jewish shepherd living among the Midianites, to approach the Pharaoh and demand freedom for his people. His simple but inspiring words, "Let my people go," continue into the present as a rallying cry for the liberation of oppressed peoples. When the Pharaoh scoffed at this lowly shepherd's plea, God responded with a series of horrific plagues: Blood (the water turned to blood), Frogs, Lice (or Vermin), Wild Beasts (or Flies), Blight (or Cattle Disease), Boils, Hail, Locusts, Darkness, and finally, Slaying of the First Born. None but the last plague convinced the Pharaoh to free the Jews, who marked their doors with lamb's blood so the Angel of Death would pass over them. The Jews fled on shaky terms and in haste. They offered sacrifices (of the Pascal lamb), and baked bread for their journey so quickly that it wasn't given time to rise. To commemorate this event, Jews eat matzo in place of bread during Passover.

Although the Jews wore no shackles, their liberation was not yet complete. Pharaoh's army pursued them as they fled toward the Red Sea. There, God performed the great miracle of splitting the Red Sea, providing safe passage on dry land for the Jewish people. But, as Pharaoh's soldiers attempted to cross after them, the waters returned, drowning the soldiers, chariots and all. Only then were the Jews able to fully embrace their freedom and toss away their chains of bondage. Having just witnessed this spectacular miracle, they spontaneously celebrated their new-found freedom, erupting into a song in praise of God.

Passover celebrates this history. The account of the Exodus, both the memory of slavery as well as the jubilation of liberation, gives Passover its structure and meaning. The events of the Exodus occurred essentially in three parts: the bitter enslavement, the crossing of the Red Sea, and the subsequent rejoicing. Passover duly reflects this pattern. Like Sukkot, Passover is subdivided into first, intermediate, and concluding days. The intermediate period is not observed in the traditional sense, but bridges the more formally observed days that lie before and after it. The initial two days are characterized by rituals and practices, including the fulfillment of the biblical commandment to eat matzo. The latter days stand in sharp contrast, maintaining similar status but requiring no specific religious commandments. While the former days may boast of two lavish meals, steeped in ritual and celebration, the latter appear, on the surface, to lack any such decoration.

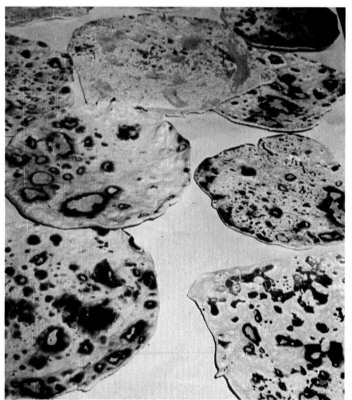

In fact, the two sides of Passover reflect an essential duality in Judaism, manifest in two distinct approaches to celebration and observance. One clearly outlines a format for celebration. The other, more subjective approach, charges the individual to shape and interpret the holiday's meaning. This duality is reflected in the seder. The very word, *seder*, means "order." Three distinct sequences make up the evening's events. The meal divides the two principle parts much the way the intermediate days of Passover divide the entire holiday. While the first section is filled with text and formal ritual, the latter allows for greater independence and urges the participants to invigorate the proceedings. This is but one sense in which the seder serves as a microcosm of the Passover holiday.

Matzo, unleavened bread for the "Seder," above, *must be watched over from the time the grain begins to grow to when the product is baked or boxed. Jews may eat no other grain product during Passover.*

The Seder Table

One may consider the seder the central event of Passover. It is not unusual for families to begin preparations days in advance, for much must be done before they gather around the handsomely set table, where freshly polished silver and sparkling crystal add to the light of the traditional candelabrum. Three matzot, placed in the center of the table, become the focus of the evening's activities. Early in the seder the leader breaks one of the matzo in two. One half is left on the table; the other—the *afikomen*—is hidden. On a simple level, this tradition encourages children to participate; the child who finds the hidden matzo wins a special gift. Symbolically, this upholds the duality of Passover. The matzo half that remains revealed functions primarily during the discussion portion of the seder and is pointed to often as a catalyst for discussion. The hidden matzo serves as a reminder of the internal element and symbolizes what lies within the individual that he or she must give expression to. When the afikomen is returned to the table, the meal is over and the seder proceeds with the songs and poetry. It is the last thing we eat during the seder, a final reminder of the personal—subjective—responsibilities of the seder.

Customarily, the family prepares a separate plate, often referred to as the "seder plate," with five symbolic foods. The plate contains a *bitter herb*—either romaine lettuce, watercress, or freshly grated horseradish—to symbolize the bitter affliction of the slavery in Egypt. A *shankbone*, symbolic of the sacrificial Pascal offering, is set beside a *roasted egg*, which represents the festival offering in the period of the Holy Temple. A green vegetable, or *sweet herb*, for dipping in salt water reminds celebrants of their ancestor's tears. *Charoses* is prepared to resemble—in appearance—the mortar of the bricks used to build the ancient Egyptian cities. This array of symbolic foods is traditionally set on a decorative ceremonial platter—the seder plate.

Aesthetics from the Old World

Beauty plays an important role in the seder. The seder plate is but one of the many objects that has engendered a history of ceremonial art. For centuries, Jewish artisans and craftsmen have designed and fashioned objects used specifically for Passover. One may find decorated saucers used to dip the herbs, embroidered cloths to cover the matzo, and carved wooden book stands to hold the *haggadah,* the book that contains all the blessings, stories, and songs recited at the seder.

During the seder the head of the table pours four cups of wine to represent the four stages of the Exodus: freedom, deliverence, redemption, and release. As a result, wine cups of varied materials and shapes often find their way to the table. Although they are commonly made of silver, the cups are often created of brass, clay, and glass, and are engraved with appropriate blessings or quotations from the Old Testament. The "Cup of Elijah," which tends to stand out as the most elegant and beautiful goblet on the table, is poured as a fifth cup, symbolic of future redemption. More and more families are using this time to address the contemporary crises that face the Jewish people, adding prayers for the redemption of Jews imprisoned in the Soviet Union and others imprisoned because of political strife the world over. A prayer for the gift of peace for the whole earth makes the moment even more special.

The Haggadah

The haggadah, the blueprint for the seder, holds the very essence and meaning of the Passover celebration. It is divided into three distinguishable sections. The first part, called *maggid*, from which the haggadah derives its name, means, "telling." In part, it is devoted to discussing the historical events that make up the story of the Exodus. In addition, it includes stories, Talmudic passages, and anecdotes that together paint a picture of how the story of the Exodus was transmitted through the ages. The haggadah itself stresses the importance of the seder as a spectacle meant to excite the interest and curiosity of children. The biblical phrase, "And you shall tell your son on the day saying . . ." (Exodus 13:8), calls upon the parents to educate their children about their history. Oral history, now written, attests to the Jews' necessary commitment to the perpetuation of their heritage from one generation to the next. Thus, the participants not only read about the Exodus, but are encouraged to dramatically relive the experience.

This segment of the seder encourages historical reflection through the use of symbols and ritual. The wide array of symbols present on the seder table are intended to incite queries as to what they indeed represent. For example, one of the first passages in the haggadah instructs the leader of the seder to point to the matzo and recite, "This is the poor man's bread which our fathers ate in the land of Egypt." The child then recites the question, "How is this night different from all other nights?" The remainder of the maggid responds to the child's question, which is one of the Four Questions that explains the symbolism within the holiday. On the seder night, all participants, regardless of age or scholarship, are equally required to relearn the history and consider

anew its meaning. And on this night especially, Jews are commanded to invite strangers who have no place to celebrate the seder into their homes. The haggadah evokes images of the countless number of Jews who have gathered around the seder table in all eras, in comfort and in poverty, in safety or in fear for their lives.

This emphasis upon history and memory also finds its source in the biblical account. The text in the Book of Exodus appears uncharacteristically repetitive in its injunction to both *remember* and *observe* the night of Passover, which is referred to as "the night of observance." The phrase, however, is accorded yet another, less familiar, meaning: "the night of anticipation." These two interpretations of this single word in the Bible hold the key to the apparent duality in the seder and in Passover as a whole. While "observance" and rememberance gesture towards the past, as does the first section of the seder, "anticipation" suggests looking to the future. And hope and anticipation are what the section following the seder meal is all about.

The group of songs collectively referred to as the Hallel and a variety of other songs and poems constitute the latter part of the seder. While the blessings and readings in the first part of the seder take the form of prose, of story telling, this portion of the haggadah takes the form of poetry. Almost all of the latter part is sung or chanted. The spirit of song leads back to the historical past as well. The Bible recounts how, after successfully crossing the Red Sea, Moses led the people in a song in praise of God called *Az Yashir*, "Then He Sang." According to Talmudic sources, the Israelites then responded with songs called *Birkat Hashir*, also known as "Hallel." Appropriately, the Hallel is the focus of much of the concluding haggadah text. Thus, the very make-up of the seder reinforces the two approaches—objective and subjective—to observance and celebration.

One of the more popular haggadahs is A Passover Haggadah, *right*, *prepared by the Central Conference of American Rabbis. The uncommonly beautiful illustrations are by renowned artist Leonard Baskin. At* **left**, *the leader of the Seder lifts one of the three ceremonial matzos from under the matzo cover.*

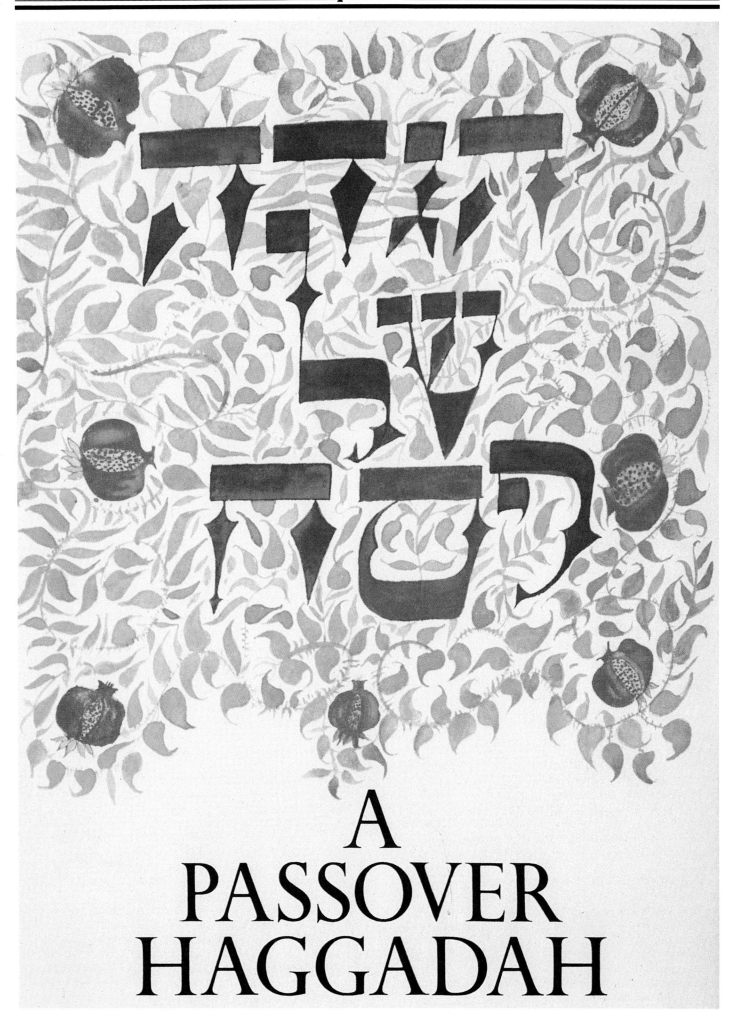

A PASSOVER HAGGADAH

The Celebrants

By S. Y. Agnon
Translated by I. M. Lask

This is the tale of Mechel, the beadle. When Mechel, the beadle, left the House of Study on the first night of Passover his mood was cheerful. Blest be The Name, said he to himself, that the Eve of Passover is over and done with so that I too can rejoice this night like other folk. But when he had locked the doors and found himself proceeding homeward his good mood left him. He knew that he went to no royal feasting hall but to a tumbledown dwelling; that he would be sitting not on a fine handsome couch but on a torn cushion unmended of woman's hand; and that he must trouble himself a deal to warm his food.

For at the time Mechel, the beadle, was a widower; there was no woman in his home to prepare his table, make his bed or cook his meals. Truth to tell, many of the householders had wished to invite him to celebrate the Passover feasts with them. Reb Mechel, they had said, tonight the whole world is rejoicing and all Israel feasts with their households, so why should you celebrate on your own? Be happy, Reb Mechel, that the demons have no power this night; but even so there is a peril of sadness, which is as much prohibited on the Passover as leaven, the Merciful One deliver us. Yet Mechel refused all offers of hospitality, for he did not wish to burden another's table at the festival.

The streets had emptied, and all the houses of the town shone with Passover light. The moon was bright and gracious, and a spring breeze blew. Mechel began to turn his mind away from himself and enjoy the wonders of the Creation, jingling the keys of the synagogue like a bell. But hearing the sound of the keys he grew sorrowful and began to remind himself bitterly how he was the beadle of the House of Study, toiling hard and doing all sorts of work; and how, when he had completed his work and returned home, he remained cramped and lonely between the walls, never even tasting cooked food; since if he put food on to warm he would be asleep before it was cooked. So he would stay his hunger with an onion roll or some bread and radish, or the potato a woman might bring to the House of Study so that he should pray for the souls of her near ones to rest in peace. But what you may do all the year round, and rest satisfied, you may not do on a festival when we are bidden to rejoice.

On the way home he noticed that one house had a window open; looking again, he saw that it was a window in the house of Sarah Leah, the widow. She herself was standing at the window looking out. Mechel bowed to her with the greeting, Festivals for joy, Sarah Leah. Holidays and appointed times for gladness, Reb Mechel, responded Sarah Leah. Whence and whither, Reb Mechel? I am coming from the House of Study, said Mechel, on my way home to prepare my table and sit and celebrate. Sarah Leah nodded her head and sighed. I see she would like to say something to me, said Mechel to himself, and stood waiting.

Seeing Mechel standing waiting, she said, I just opened my window to see if it were time to leave, for I am celebrating at my neighbor's. I've prepared all sorts of good things, by your life, and I'm short of nothing in order to celebrate the Passover down to the last detail, and all the same I have to leave my own home and burden myself on others. It's not enough that I go burdening them every Sabbath and festival, when I suddenly appear among them for the Hallowing and the Havdala; I have to go bothering them on Passover as well.

Well, it may be a bother in your eyes, said Mechel, but others regard it as fulfilling a commandment. A commandment, d'you say, Reb Mechel, responded Sarah Leah. Do you suppose such commandments come easily to those who perform them? Here's a man who's busy all day long and never sees his wife and children; Passover comes, a time of rest; he wishes to sit quiet with his family when in jumps that widow all of a sudden and sits down among them. May it be His Will that I shouldn't sin with my words, the years grow less and the world grows wearier and weaker. In times gone by a Jew would bring any number of guests home with him and there'd be room enough; and nowadays there's no room even for a lonely widow like me. I remember Passover at Father's, may he rest in peace, when we'd have ten Jews and more there. And was my husband, may he rest in peace, accustomed to celebrate Passover without a guest? And I have to leave my home now. And am I short of anything here? If it's wine a body wants, here's wine and enough to spare for an extra glass; and if it's matzoth, here are the extra special matzoth; if it's meat, here's a turkey cock whose wings were absolutely hidden by fat. Why, what did the neighbors say, Sarah Leah, don't tie him to the foot of your bed or he'll drag you across Sambatyon River That's no bird, that's an aurochs. But as long as a woman's in her husband's house it's all worthwhile; and once he's dead even the whole of the world isn't worthwhile. At first I was thinking of inviting a guest, only folk would say, That old woman's a fiend from Hell, wants a man for to serve her well.

Mechel smiled, signed and quoted the Talmud, " 'Tis better to dwell in trouble than to dwell in widowhood." And although the saying was in Aramaic, a tongue Sarah Leah did not understand, she nodded her head like a person saying, You've said it well and true. Mechel's an upright man and assuredly has some good thought in mind. And she added, There's everything here, but if there's no master in the house what is there in the house? I often ask myself, Sarah Leah, what are you doing here and whom have you here? I have reared children to their full size and they forsook me, so now I am bereft and forsaken, as a table after a feast. I thought of ascending to the Land of Israel to be near the holy places, and not be thinking all the time of my loneliness; but then I am again faced by the difficulty, how can a woman go alone to a place where she is not known? All Israel are brethren, but nevertheless my heart troubles me at the thought of ascending alone.

Mechel felt full of pity for her. He took hold of his right earlock and wished to say words of comfort to her. Yet he could get nothing out, began stammering and at last said, Woman, is my luck any greater than yours? You, God be praised, are adorned as a bride and eat fine food, while I am chidden and mourning as a widower. But no man in Israel has other to depend on than the loving kindness of the Holy and Blest One. What has any living person to grumble at? The festival should not be degraded.

And from seeking to comfort her he began to feel sorry for himself and he said, And what is a man? Something bare in the waste. Blest be He that did not make me a woman. Blest be His Name that I know how to hallow the wine and prepare for the Passover according to the law. But now go to a tumbledown dwelling and warm up half-cooked food and sit on a broken bed, and then sit on a torn cushion and think you're like a king. It was with good reason the Yalkut says, All sufferings are hard to bear, but those of poverty are hardest of all; all sufferings come, and once they are gone leave things as they were; but poverty dims the eyes of a man. I'm only saying this to balance your saying, I'm a woman. And what's more the Holy and Blest One has brought a bad cough upon me, may you never know its like, which takes away my breath and steals the life from me and will drive me out of the world. And before ever he finished speaking he had begun coughing. Reb Mechel, said Sarah Leah to him, don't stand out in the cold; winter may have gone but it's still chilly. Better come into the house and not stand about in the open.

Mechel bowed his head between his shoulders, entered and found himself in a fine dwelling with handsomely decked cushions to recline upon, and a table covered with silverware in the middle of the room, and a bottle of wine on the table, candles burning in all the candlesticks and every corner of the room gleaming and shining with festival. His first words were in honor of the place, for he said, How fine this room is, where the hands of a woman have been employed. Sarah Leah at once rushed to show him all she had ready for the table. Matzoth and bitter herbs lay there, parsley and *haroseth,* eggs and a sheepshank and flesh and fish and a fat pudding and borsht red as wine.

And who, said Sarah Leah to Mechel, needs all this array? I'm just about to go off and bother somebody else, but it's hard for me to forget that I'm a housewife, so I prepared a Passover for myself as though my husband were still there and he and I were celebrating like all other folk.

Mechel's heart warmed within him, and he wished to say something, but a furious fit of coughing overcame him. Sarah Leah stared at him with her two eyes and said, Don't eat too much bitter herbs and don't eat sharp foods, Reb Mechel; you cough too badly. You know what you need? It's a glass of hot tea you need. But who have you at home to make something hot? Wait a few moments and I'll put the kettle on for you.

But scarce had she finished her sentence when she struck herself on the mouth, crying, What a silly head I have, to forget that we have to hallow the festival first. Maybe you'll celebrate here? And since the thought had found expression in words she repeated, Maybe you'll celebrate here? Mechel saw all the goodness of the housewife and could not move, as though his limbs were fastened to the spot where he stood. He began stammering and swallowed his indistinct answer. And

Sarah Leah began preparing the feast as had been her wont when her husband was still with her.

So Mechel took the keys of the House of Study and put them away somewhere, staring meanwhile at the white cushions that Sarah Leah had prepared for reclining on during the celebration as though the Higher Light shone from them. Within a few moments he had let himself down among them, by reason of the thought that the woman would again ask him to celebrate with her. When she saw him at his ease she filled a glass with wine. With one eye on the wine and one on the household ware, he thought to himself, What a fine spot this is, where a woman's hands do the tending. While thinking, he found the glass of wine at his hand, and his lips of themselves began repeating the hallowing of the wine.

Sarah Leah sighed with satisfaction; her face grew bright; her clothes were suddenly filled with her body, as happens with a rejoicing person; and she thought to herself, How fine is a Jew's voice when he utters holy words. And within a moment she had brought him a ewer of water. He washed his hands, took a leaf of greenstuff, dipped it in salt water, broke the matzoth in half, put one half in a cloth and hid it away for the dessert, lifted up the dish and began reciting, "This is the bread of affliction, that which our fathers ate in the Land of Egypt."

And Sarah Leah wondered at herself, saying, Just a little while ago I was preparing to leave my house, and now here am I sitting at home. And she watched Mechel's hands, observing how accustomed his hands were in holy things, until her face grew red and she lowerered her eyes in shame. Then she filled the glasses afresh and uncovered the matzoth. Mechel made her a sign. Sarah Leah blushed like a child, dropped her eyes to the prayer book and recited the Four Questions to their close, "This night we all do recline." Thereupon Mechel set the dish back in place and repeated in a loud and joyful voice, "We were the slaves of Pharaoh in Egypt"; and he continued reciting the Relation of the Departure from Egypt as far as the feast, interpreting to her in Yiddish all that required interpretation and seasoning the entire Relation with parables and tales of wonder. His sufferings and troubles far from him, his head resting on the cushion, sweat caressing his earlocks and the cushion growing deeper beneath him, he continued. His blood beat through his limbs and his heart might have leapt forth; a single hour here was preferable to his whole life in This World.

The Order of Passover came to its appointed end.

Ehad Mi Yodea?

E - - had - - mi yo - dĕ - a?_____ E_____- had a -

ni yo - dĕ - a: E - had el - lo - hĕ - nu, e - lo - hĕ - nu, e - lo - hĕ - nu, e -

lo - hĕ - nu, e - lo - hĕ - nu, e - lo_ - hĕ_ - nu, she - ba - sha - ma - yim

u - va - a - rets,_____ She - ba - sha - ma - yim u - va - a - rets.

Seder 5732

There stands Mr. Cohen
octogenarianly balanced.
  survivor, refugee, immigrant, naturalized
    U.S. citizen
  fifty years a kosher butcher
  on Bond Street
  in Baltimore
  in the ghetto
  which then meant Jewish
peering at his grandsons
  precious probes
  orbiting into time
glancing at his son
  course fixed
  for re-entry into forgetfullness
for clues
as he gropes for the sequence
of events
his grandsons may never know existed
even before their father
was a little boy.

There sits Mr. Cohen
ceremonially clad
a hibernating figure
visited on a legendary night
stared at by grandsons
blushing indignation as stories are told
by the gathered clan
of events they can't remember
when they were little boys
and eons passed between
one matzo eating time
and the next
recounting of the deliverance of Abraham's heirs
in the mysterious meaningless sounds
chanted by the grownups
until unleashed to let Elijah in
taste the wine and hunt for afikomen
and proudly read aloud the playful
  English rhymes of
"I have one. . . ."

       —JOSEPH ROBERT COHEN

The Sound of Seders

Family group at table
  changes year to year
  some born some gone
  different faces here
But the blessings never change
No the blessings never change
  I hear my father's voice

Family roles at service shift
  Time moves us up the stairs
  to another generation
  other members lead the prayers
But the blessings never change
No the blessings never change
  I feel my father's melody

And with each ringing memory
  of syllable and song
  I taste my father's music

      —REE GOODMAN

Had Gadya

One little goat, one little goat
My father bought for two zuzim.
One little goat, one little goat.

Then came a cat and ate the goat
My father bought for two zuzim.
One little goat, one little goat.

Then came a dog and bit the cat that ate the goat
My father bought for two zuzim.
One little goat, one little goat.

Then came a stick and beat the dog that bit the cat
That ate the goat
My father bought for two zuzim.
One little goat, one little goat.

Then came a fire and burnt the stick that beat the dog
That bit the cat that ate the goat
My father bought for two zuzim.
One little goat, one little goat.

Then water came and quenched the fire that burnt the stick
That beat the dog that bit the cat that ate the goat
My father bought for two zuzim.
One little goat, one little goat.

Then came an ox and drank the water that quenched the fire
That burnt the stick that beat the dog
That bit the cat that ate the goat
My father bought for two zuzim.
One little goat, one little goat.

Then came a slaughterer and slaughtered the ox that drank the water
That quenched the fire that burnt the stick that beat the dog
That bit the cat that ate the goat
My father bought for two zuzim.
One little goat, one little goat.

Then came the Angel of Death and slew the slaughterer
Who slaughtered the ox that drank the water that quenched the fire
That burnt the stick that beat the dog that bit the cat
That ate the goat
My father bought for two zuzim.
One little goat, one little goat.

Then came the Holy One, Blessed be He, and smote the Angel of Death
Who slew the slaughterer who slaughtered the ox that drank the water
That quenched the fire that burnt the stick that beat the dog
That bit the cat that ate the goat
My father bought for two zuzim.
One little goat, one little goat.

Dayenu

II. I-lu na-tan, na-tan la-nu,
   Na-tan la-nu To-rat e-met,
   To-rat e-met na-tan la-nu,
   da-ye-nu.
   chorus

The Seder

The rules governing Passover are strict and many. No utensils, dishes, or crockery used in the preparation for the Festival must be used during Passover itself; separate utensils and dishware are kept for use only during Passover. No leavened foods or grains are allowed in the house. Nor are packages of food that have been opened before Passover. All remaining foodstuffs that are prohibited during Passover must be disposed of before a certain time in the morning on the eve of the Festival (for complete rules, consult your local rabbi). So cooks must turn to using matzo meal, potato starch, and fresh and speciality foods. The menu given below updates the traditional meal. Smoked fish, which you can buy at a delicatessen, is recommended instead of gefilte fish. The chicken soup is flavoured with dill, and bitter herbs wind up in the salad as well as on the Seder plate. The citrus sponge cake made with matzo meal is surprisingly light and airy. You may even want to serve it as dessert on another holiday, with whipped cream and raspberries as topping.

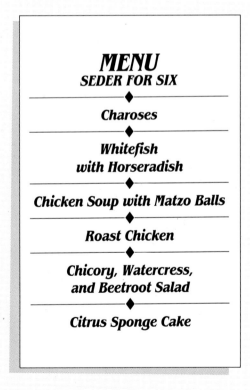

MENU
SEDER FOR SIX

◆

Charoses

◆

**Whitefish
with Horseradish**

◆

Chicken Soup with Matzo Balls

◆

Roast Chicken

◆

**Chicory, Watercress,
and Beetroot Salad**

◆

Citrus Sponge Cake

Charoses (Ashkenazic Style)

1 apple, preferably tart
¼ cup chopped walnuts or pecans, or almonds
1 teaspoon honey
Dash cinnamon
Dash orange zest
1 tablespoon kosher red wine

Chop the apple to your preference. If making a fine mixture, also chop the nutmeats finely. Mix together with the honey, cinnamon, orange zest, and wine.

Charoses (Sephardic Style)

1 cup pitted dates
½ cup walnuts, pecans, or almonds
¼ teaspoon ginger
1 tablespoon kosher red wine

Soak the dates in water for approximately three hours, then simmer them for 15 minutes. Chop the nutmeats finely or put them through a food processor or grinder. Add the dates to the food processor or grinder (or chop well), then add the ginger and wine. Blend well.

Variations: Add one orange or substitute ½ cup raisins for ½ cup of the dates.

Matzo Balls

3 eggs
3 tablespoons chicken fat
½ teaspoon salt
3 tablespoons hot water or chicken soup
¾ cup matzo meal

Separate the eggs. Beat the yolks until light-colored and thick. Add the chicken fat, which should be at room temperature, and the salt and water or soup. Beat the whites until stiff but not too dry. Fold in. Fold in the matzo meal. Refrigerate the batter for about 1 hour, or until batter is thick enough to form balls.

Drop the balls carefully into 2 quarts of boiling salted water or hot soup. Cover and cook for 25 minutes. If not in the soup, put the dumplings in now. Cook for another 15 or 20 minutes in the soup.

Chicken Soup

4 to 5 pound chicken
3 quarts cold water
1 cup carrots, cut into chunks
4 celery ribs
1 onion, quartered
2 cloves, whole
2 peppercorns
1 bay leaf
Salt to taste
Few springs fresh dill

Wipe or rinse chicken. Cut the chicken into two or four pieces depending on the size of the pot. Cover with water and bring to a boil. Add carrots, celery, onion, cloves, peppercorns, bay leaf, and salt. Simmer for 2 hours, skimming occasionally. Strain the soup and cool. Refrigerate until the fat rises to the top and can be separated from the stock.

Bring the stock to a simmer again (add knaidlech if desired) and heat for 15 or 20 minutes. Adjust seasonings to taste. To serve, pour soup into individual bowls, add knaidlech (if desired) and garnish with snipped dill.

Roast Chicken

5 pound roasting chicken
Kosher salt
¼ cup melted chicken fat or vegetable oil
Pepper to taste
½ tablespoon dried tarragon
Few sprigs fresh tarragon, if available

Preheat the oven to 450°F. Wipe or rinse the chicken inside and out. Cut off any extra fat and set aside. Rub with kosher salt inside and out. Brush the outside of the chicken with vegetable or melted chicken fat. Sprinkle pepper and tarragon over the bird. Place a few sprigs of fresh tarragon, if available, inside the cavity. Put the chicken on the rack of an uncovered roasting pan, breast side up. Soak a piece of cheesecloth in melted chicken fat or vegetable oil. Cover the breast of the chicken with the cheesecloth. Place in the preheated oven and reduce heat to 350°F. Baste with pan juices about every 15 minutes. (Make sure to soak the cloth or go under the cloth when basting.) Bake for 1¾ to 2 hours. Remove the cheesecloth after 1¼ hours.

Endive, Watercress, and Beet Salad

3 heads of Belgian endive

3 bunches of watercress

3 beets

Wash the endive and trim it. Rinse the watercress and break off any brown stems. Bring enough water to a boil so that it will half cover the beets. Cut the tops off and wash the beets. Place them in the boiling water, reduce the heat to a simmer, and cook covered for 40 minutes, or until tender. Rinse the cooked beets under cold tap water, then slip off the skins. Slice into matchstick-size pieces.

Arrange the endive, stem-side down, tops up, in a glass bowl. Make a bed of watercress, then arrange the cut beets on top of the watercress.

Lime Dressing

Juice of 3 limes

1 teaspoon lemon juice

¼ teaspoon salt

Dash of white pepper

4 tablespoons olive oil

Combine the lime juice, lemon juice, and salt and pepper to taste. Whisk to blend, then add the oil as you continue to whisk. When well-mixed, pour over the salad.

Citrus Sponge Cake

½ cup unsalted matzo cake meal

¼ cup potato starch

Zest of 1 lemon

Zest of ½ orange

6 eggs

1 cup sugar

3 teaspoons fresh lemon juice

2 teaspoons fresh orange juice

Pinch of salt

Preheat oven to 350°F.

Sift the matzo meal and potato starch together three times; set aside. Grate the zest of the lemon and half the orange; set aside.

Bring the eggs to room temperature, separate, then beat the yolks until they are light-colored and thick, about two minutes with an electric mixer at moderate speed. Gradually add approximately two-thirds of the sugar to the yolks, beating constantly. Add the lemon juice, orange juice, and lemon and orange rinds; beat until well mixed. In a separate bowl, beat the whites with the salt until they begin to foam, then add the remaining sugar and beat until the whites are stiff and dry.

Fold the matzo meal mixture into the yolk mixture. Blend well. Then fold the egg whites into the batter and blend well. Pour into an ungreased tube pan and bake for one hour.

Test by checking the interior of the cake with a tester or broomstraw, which should come out clean. Cool the cake by inverting the pan on a bottle. Do not remove the cake from the pan until it is completely cooled.

Matzo Cover

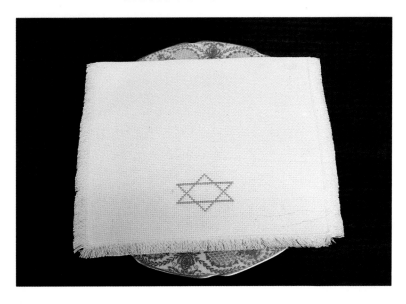

Materials:

*#14 Aida cloth (a cotton even-weave fabric
   designed for cross-stitch that has 14
   squares to the inch)*
Gold embroidery floss
Small embroidery hoop
Embroidery needle
Zigzag sewing machine for binding edges

A beautiful heirloom matzo cover can be
assembled and decorated with embroidery
in a project that is not tremendously time-
consuming. The Aida cloth, which is also
used for the Chanukah placemats and napkins, is a fabric with beautiful texture and
durability.

Cutting and Stitching the Seams

The matzo cover can be made from one
piece of fabric, folded and stitched to provide three pockets for the matzo. Cut a
piece of Aida cloth to measure 10″ wide and
32″ long. Sew a plain zigzag border around
the perimeter of the fabric, ½″ away from
the edge.

Cross-Stitching the Design

Using the cross-stitch methods described in
the Chanukah placemat project, cross-stitch
a simple Star-of-David motif on one edge of
the fabric, centered, and 1 inch from the
zigzag border (illus. 5A)

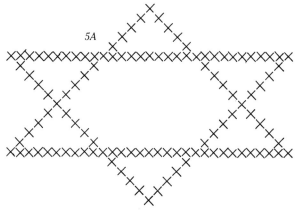

5A

Then, fold the cloth, as illustrated, to
create three pockets. The finished measurement of the folded matzo cover will now be
10″ x 8″ (illus. 5B).

5B

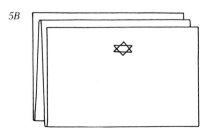

Complete the edges by fringing. By
hand, remove one thread at a time until you
have come to the zigzag border. Iron to
crease folds, and stitch the ends about a half
inch away from the fringed edges (illus. 5C).

5C

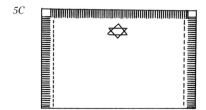

Materials:

#14 Aida cloth
Embroidery cotton floss (6 strand)
Embroidery needle
Small embroidery hoop
*Optional: Graph paper with ⅛″ squares, if
   you would like to design additional
   motifs or monograms*
Yardstick or meterstick
Pencil
Sewing machine

Determining the Sizes of Your Placemats and Napkins

Decide how many placemats and napkins
you would like to stitch, and what their
finished size will be. The average placemat
size is 11″ x 17″, and a good napkin size is
15″ square. Cut out sample placemats from
newsprint and lay them out on your dining
room table. This will show you whether the
number of place settings fits comfortably on
the table without overlapping.

Before Cutting the Fabric

Preshrink the fabric first by washing. Use
your paper pattern of the placemat to see
how you can best lay out the placemats and
napkins without fabric waste. Use pins as
markers and, if your eyesight requires it,
lightly draw the placemat and napkin outlines on the fabric. Since they are going to
be fringed according to the woven grain of
the fabric, *it is very important that your
cutting lines be exactly on the line of the
weave. It is also very important that you
trim off the approximately ½″ selvage
(woven edge) of the fabric before laying out
your pattern shapes. Selvage is too tightly
woven to be turned into fringe.*

Preparing the Placemats & Napkins for Cross-Stitch

Using your sewing machine, stitch a border
around the perimeter of the placemat, using
the same thread color as your placemat. If
you have a zigzag attachment, stitch for one
round, making the pattern stitch the width
of one square. If using a straight stitch, sew
two parallel rows around the perimeter of
the mat. Keep the stitching ⅝″ away from
and strictly parallel with the edge. At each
corner, stop and carefully pivot the fabric—
making a right angle—so that you don't pull
the corners too tightly. The purpose of this
machine-stitched border is to prevent the
fabric from unraveling.

Color Choices

Fabric and thread choices can be made on
the basis of your own decorating scheme at
home, or in terms of the holiday colors you
wish to convey. Our instructions here have
the colors listed according to the illustration
samples (see illus. 5D).

Beginning to Cross-Stitch

Separate a 15″ piece of floss into individual
strands and then put 3 strands together—

Placemat and Napkin Set

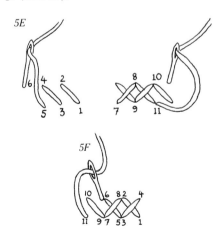

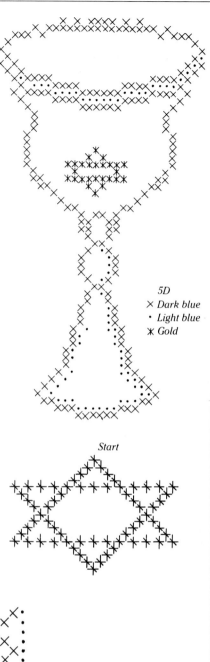

5D
× Dark blue
• Light blue
✳ Gold

Start

straight—to make a stitching length. Thread your needle and begin with the border of the placemat. It is rather awkward to fit the placemat on an embroidery hoop and have it positioned for the border. You'll find that although you need to move the hoop frequently, this method *does* produce the smoothest stitches. You can choose not to use the embroidery hoop when stitching the border, but it will mean being especially careful to keep your stitches even.

Crosses are made in two ways: You can stitch all of the crosses in one direction first (illus. 5E) and then go back and stitch the other direction of the cross (illus. 5E). Or, you may stitch each cross completely as you go (illus. 5F).

5E

5F

The Aida cloth is woven so that it has "holes" in between tiny woven squares. These holes are where you insert your needle, and the squares determine the size of the crosses. The results are perfectly placed crosses and an impeccable appearance for your design.

Never use knots in your stitching. Begin the cross-stitching by bringing the needle down through the fabric about 2″ away from your beginning stitch and coming up through the fabric to begin the cross (illus. 5G).

5G

As you proceed in the direction of your thread end, your stitches will catch the end of the floss on the backside. Carefully trim off the end that is showing on the front. When the floss is too short to use, carefully draw the needle under about an inch of crosses *on the back of the work* and trim the end. If the thread becomes twisted at any time, let the needle hang loose and untwist itself.

Suggested Motifs

We have chosen Elijah's Cup as the motif for our placemats, and a Star-of-David for the napkins. Other symbols and monograms may be used to personalize them. If you would like to translate a favorite motif into a cross-stitch design, use the graph paper and a pencil to lay out the main outline. Then, add the detail inside the shape as you wish. Use a different symbol (dot, cross, solid) for each color represented.

Stitching the Motifs

With the border completed, carefully count your squares to begin the main motif in the correct position. Then proceed to stitch, using the main color first. The bottom left

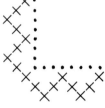

corner of the cup is 25 spaces from the bottom border and 24 spaces from the left side border. (See arrow in illus. 5D).

The napkins do not have borders, so simply count the squares to center the Star-of-David on the corner, and stitch. This one is 1½″ from the corner.

Finishing Details

Complete the placemat and napkins by fringing the edges. By hand, carefully remove one thread at a time until you have come to the zigzag border.

Do not pull out more than one thread at a time or the threads will break and bunch up. With the border fringed, iron and starch your placemat for a professional finished look.

SHAVUOT

The Feast of Weeks

Shavuot, the Feast of Weeks, is an agricultural holiday celebrating the harvest season in Israel. The name *Shavuot* ("weeks") refers to the timing of the festival, which is held exactly seven weeks after Passover. The Torah calls Shavuot *Yom Habikkurim,* "the day of the first fruits," because farmers would bring the first of their harvest to Jerusalem as a token of thanksgiving to God. Shavuot also commemorates the anniversary of the giving of the Ten Commandments at Mount Sinai.

Along with Passover and Sukkot, Shavuot is one of the *Shalosh Regalim,* the three pilgrimage holidays on which, in ancient times, all the Jews would journey to Jerusalem and worship at the Temple. Today, the celebration of Shavuot centers around the home and synagogue.

A Harvest Festival

In ancient Israel the harvest season began in the spring —with Passover—when the barley crop was harvested. In the months that followed, the other crops and fruits began to ripen. The very first ripe fruits of each species were called *bikkurim.*

When a Jewish farmer saw the first cluster of grapes or the first pomegranate or the first ripe figs, he would not pluck the fruit and eat it. Instead, the farmer would tie a ribbon around the branch of the fruit. This ribbon served as a sign to all that these fruits were bikkurim, first fruits, to be brought to Jerusalem and eaten in the Holy City.

Every farmer would gather his bikkurim in a basket and set out on his journey to Jerusalem. On the road he would meet other farmers bearing the bikkurim they had grown. Those who lived near Jerusalem brought fresh fruit, while farmers traveling a long distance carried raisins and dried figs, which would not spoil during the trip.

Although the bikkurim ritual is no longer practiced, fresh fruits and vegetables ,right, are still very much associated with Shavuot.

The pilgrims, led by flute players, carried their baskets on their shoulders. Every basket was adorned with decorative fruits specially chosen for their beauty. As the procession neared Jerusalem, a spirit of anticipation and excitement seized the travelers; they raised their voices in song, and their march became a dance.

At the outskirts of the city, the president and officers of the Temple stood waiting to greet the pilgrims. Sometimes the king himself emerged and joined the procession. Together, everyone marched toward the Temple Mount. On the steps of the Temple, the Levites sang welcome to the travelers.

Then each farmer would present his basket to a Temple priest and recite the following declaration:

> My ancestor was a stranger when he went down to Egypt, but there he became a great and strong nation. Then the Egyptians afflicted and enslaved us. So God brought us out of Egypt with a mighty hand and glorious miracles. And He gave us this land, a land flowing with milk and honey. And now, behold, I have brought the first of the fruit of the land which God has given me.

The bikkurim ritual, though no longer practiced today, represents a pertinent moral lesson: the acknowledgement that one's accomplishments and success depend on factors beyond one's control. The farmer gave thanks to God for a bountiful harvest. We, too, should recognize the good fortune in our lives and demonstrate our gratefulness on Shavuot.

The Ten Commandments

After escaping from Egypt the Children of Israel found themselves wandering in the hot desert wilderness. But God provided them with water to drink and manna to curb their hunger. At the end of two long months, the people camped at the foot of a great mountain named Sinai. Although surrounded by a dry, bare desert, Mount Sinai was green and lush, covered with flowers, grass, and trees.

On the third day of the Hebrew month of Sivan, God commanded Moses to prepare the Jewish people. Every person was required to wash and purify his body and cleanse his clothing to ready himself. For in three days God Himself would descend and speak to the entire nation, man, woman, and child. When Moses brought this message to the people, they answered as one: "Everything that God has said, we will do."

Three days later, on the morning of the sixth day of Sivan, the people woke to thunder and lightning. A thick, black cloud hung over the mountain. The sounds of the *shofar,* the ram's horn, echoed over the desert. The earth itself began to tremble and shake. Suddenly, a voice, God's voice, spoke out of the clouds:

"I am the Lord your God who brought you out of slavery from the land of Egypt.

"You shall have no other gods but me.

"You shall not take the name of your Lord in vain.

"You shall remember and keep the Sabbath day holy.

"Honor your father and mother.

"You shall not kill.

"You shall not commit adultery.

"You shall not steal.

"You shall not bear false witness against your neighbor.

"You shall not covet your neighbor's wife, nor anything that belongs to your neighbor."

And the First Tablets were received.

Through the centuries the Jewish people have celebrated this climactic event. At Sinai a worn and weary throng of former slaves was transformed into a nation called Israel. The Ten Commandments became the foundation of Jewish law and the moral standard of the entire world.

Customs and Legends

Many traditional Shavuot customs stem from legends describing the experience at Sinai. For instance, according to tradition, on the morning of the first Shavuot, when God Himself would declare the Ten Commandments to the people, the Children of Israel actually overslept! To compensate for their negligence, Jews the world over have adopted a vigil on Shavuot eve. From dusk to dawn they remain awake, occupying themselves with the study of Torah and Talmud. A digest has evolved, called _Tikkun Leil Shavuot_, or the "Restoration of Shavuot Eve," which spans the breadth of rabbinic literature, including selections from Torah, the Prophets, Talmud, and the Zohar, the foundation of Jewish mysticism. Despite its length many still recite the Tikkun Leil Shavuot. However, most who choose to sacrifice their sleep on Shavuot eve concentrate their study on those texts that they find particularly interesting and exciting.

Another custom related to Shavuot is the eating of dairy foods. Some consider this practice an allusion to the verse in the Torah quoted by the farmer at the conclusion of his pilgrimage: "And He gave us this land, a land flowing with milk and honey." Others offer an explanation based on the following legend: Before receiving the Torah on Shavuot, the Jewish people were not bound by the Kashrut (dietary) laws; they ate pork and other non-kosher meats. On Shavuot they first learned of these restrictions, which rendered all of their utensils non-kosher and unfit for use. Without kosher meat and utensils, the Children of Israel had no choice but to eat dairyfoods. Today, in commemoration of this, Jews eat blintzes, cheesecake, and other dairy dishes.

Some experts attribute the tradition of eating dairy foods , above, on Shavuot to the biblical quotation: "And He gave us this land, a land flowing with milk and honey." Planting trees on Shavuot, a custom adopted in some congregations, celebrates the summer harvest.

Legend has it that Mount Sinai bloomed in expectation of God's revelation. The lush, green mountain stood out proudly in the middle of the desert. From this tradition grew the custom to decorate the synagogue and Jewish homes with tree branches and flowers. Some lay wreaths of roses on the Torah scrolls as well. The greenery recalls the natural splendor of Sinai on the first Shavuot in history.

Since the days of the Talmud, Jews have customarily read the Book of Ruth on Shavuot day. Several different explanations of the connection between the Scroll of Ruth and Shavuot have been suggested. The story of Ruth unfolds during the harvest season, which coincides with Shavuot. Ruth has the distinction of being King David's great-grandmother; according to tradition David was born and died on Shavuot. Finally, Ruth's conversion to Judaism parallels the experience of the entire Jewish people at Sinai, when they accepted God and His Ten Commandments.

Another text associated with Shavuot is an Aramaic poem called *Akdamut*. Written in the eleventh century by the German poet, Rabbi Meir ben Isaac of Worms, *Akdamut* serves as an introduction to the Ten Commandments. With rich imagery the poem describes God's creation of the world, the song of the angels, and the greatness and suffering of the Jewish people. *Akdamut* is comprised of ninety lines; the first forty-four form a double acrostic of the Hebrew alphabet. The first letters of the remaining lines spell out the name of the author and the following blessing: "May he grow in Torah and in good deeds, amen. Be strong and have courage."

Sephardic communities do not recite *Akdamut*.

Instead, they read a poem entitled *Azharot* by Rabbi Shlomo ben Gabirol, the Spanish poet and philosopher. *Azharot* lists in rhyme all six hundred and thirteen commandments that appear, implicitly or explicitly, in the Torah.

Many old Jewish communities developed their own Shavuot customs. In Mainz, the oldest Jewish community in Germany, they would bake a special Shavuot bread called Sinai. The Sinai bread was particularly sweet to indicate the sweetness of accepting the Torah. In Frankfurt-on-the-Main in West Germany, the Jews would prepare a dish shaped like a ladder with seven steps, symbolizing the seven heavens in which God resides.

In the Middle Ages the custom developed to introduce the child to Torah study on Shavuot, as tradition held that the Torah was given on that day. At dawn the father would bring his child to the synagogue. The child sat before his teacher; between them lay a tablet with all the letters of the Hebrew alphabet. The teacher would read each letter, and the child would repeat after him. A spot of honey sat on every letter, and the child licked the honey from each letter as he learned it. The young student was then presented with a honey cake with a Torah verse written upon it. At the conclusion of the lesson, the child read the verse and ate the cake.

Shavuot combines two major elements of Jewish religious life, thanksgiving to God and devotion to the Torah. Because these concepts are inherently democratic, the holiday serves to unify the Jewish people. Shavuot affirms the Jewish heritage, while encouraging learning that is new and fresh.

The Story of Ruth

Adapted by Eli Clark

Long ago, when the Judges ruled Israel, the land of Canaan suffered a terrible famine. Elimelech, a prominent Jew from Bethlehem, took his wife, Naomi, and his two sons, Machlon and Chilion, to the land of Moab to escape the plague. The family settled in Moab, and Elimelech's sons married Moabite women, one named Orpah and the other, Ruth.

Then, tragedy struck. First Elimelech, then both of his sons, died. Naomi, suddenly a widow, told her two bereaved daughters-in-law to return to their Moabite families and find new husbands. "I shall return to Bethlehem," Naomi said and kissed them goodbye.

But Orpah and Ruth wept and said, "No, we will return with you to your people."

And Naomi said, "Turn back, my daughters. In Moab you may find a husband. I have no more sons to offer you; I have only bitterness."

So Orpah kissed her mother-in-law and left. But Ruth still refused to go. "Urge me not to leave you," Ruth said. "For where you go, I will go. Your people shall be my people, and your God shall be my God. Where you die, I will die, and there I will be buried."

Naomi saw that Ruth would not be persuaded. So together they journeyed to Bethlehem. They arrived at the beginning of the barley harvest.

At that time the custom of the Jews was to leave the grain that fell from the hands of the harvesters lying in the field. The poor were then permitted to glean the fields for fallen grain.

Ruth said to Naomi, "Let me go out to the field for grain."

"Go my daughter," Naomi replied.

The field in which Ruth gleaned belonged to Boaz, a relative of Naomi's late husband, Elimelech. Boaz noticed the young woman in his field and inquired as to who she might be. The overseer of Boaz's harvesters told him, "She is Ruth, the Moabite girl who returned with Naomi."

Boaz approached Ruth and said to her, "Do not leave and glean in the field of anyone else. Stay in my field; I have ordered my men not to disturb you. And when you become thirsty, drink of the water my men have drawn."

Ruth bowed in thanks to Boaz. "Why have I deserved this? I am a stranger in this land."

Boaz replied, "I have heard of all that you have done for Naomi, your mother-in-law; how you left your father and mother and the land of your birth. May God reward you."

At mealtime, Boaz offered Ruth to share in his lunch. Afterward, he ordered his men to drop extra grain in Ruth's path.

When Ruth returned home at the end of the day, she carried a generous amount of grain. She explained to Naomi what had occurred that day. And Naomi said, "God bless Boaz. He is a close relative. Do as he says and glean only in his field." So Ruth continued to glean in Boaz's field throughout the barley and wheat harvests.

After the harvest had ended, Naomi instructed Ruth to visit Boaz that night at his threshing-floor. "When he goes to sleep, lie down at his feet. He will tell you what to do."

When Boaz woke, he found a girl at his feet. "Who are you?" he cried.

"I am Ruth, your servant."

Boaz replied, "God bless you, for everyone knows you are a worthy woman." And Boaz, who loved Ruth, agreed to marry her. But at that time the nearest relative was entitled to marry a widow. And there was a nearer relative than Boaz.

The next morning, Boaz met this close relative at the city gate. Boaz explained, "There is a piece of land that belonged to our relative, Elimelech, which his widow, Naomi, is offering for sale. If you choose to buy it, however, you must also marry Ruth."

The relative replied, "I cannot. Therefore, you may fulfill your responsibility as the next closest relative."

So Boaz married Ruth. Nine months later Ruth gave birth to a son, named Oved. And the women of Bethlehem said to Naomi, "Bless God who has not forsaken you in old age. Your daughter-in-law who loves you has given birth to a son."

And Oved's son was Jesse, who fathered David, King of Israel.

* * * *

Why was the Scroll of Ruth written? In order to teach the rewards of those who perform deeds of kindness.

—MIDRASH

A Ketubah for Shavuot

Translated by Larry Kwass

The *ketubah* is the Jewish marriage document, stating the obligations of a husband to his wife and recording the circumstances of the wedding ceremony. In honor of Shavuot a custom existed among Sephardic communities of drawing up a *ketubah,* wedding the Torah to the people of Israel. During the synagogue service the document was read to the whole congregation. The following is part of a Shavuot *ketubah.*

With a good sign and good luck, for a time of goodwill, blessings, and success.

On the sixth of the week: He endowed Torah to His loved ones on the sixth of the month of Sivan. On that day the Eternal God came forth from Sinai and shined from Seir. He appeared on Mount Paran to all the kings of the nations in the two-thousand, four-hundred and forty-eighth year since creation of the world (according to the count we still make with song and music) in this beautiful and splendid land, the great and awesome desert. The groom, the noble among noblemen and prince of the princes is called *Israel*, a name exalted [in praise] among the nations. One is my dove to her mother. Be my wife, you who are as beautiful as the moon. I betroth you to me forever and I betroth you to me with faith.... With the help of Heaven I will work and honor you all my days, forever. I will give you the sum for a comely virgin: an ear that hears, an eye that sees. I desire that the bride, the holy *Torah*, be my wife and be inscribed on the tablet of my heart. And let a crown of royalty be placed upon her head.

בס״ד
בששי בשבת שלשה עשר יום לחדש סיון שנת חמשת אלפים
ושבע מאות שלשים ושמונה למנין שאנו מנין כאן בניו יאשעל
ניו יורק בארצות הברית באמריקה הצפונית איך הר״ר צבי בן
יהודה אמר להדא בתולתא אסתר בת חיים הוי לי לאנתו כדת
משה וישראל ואנא אפלח ואזכיר ואיזון ואפרנס יתיכי ליכי
כהלכות גוברין יהודאין דפלחין ומזכירין וזנין ומפרנסין
לנשיהון בקושטא ויהיבנא ליכי מהר בתוליכי כסף זוזי מאתן
דחזי ליכי מדאוריתא ומזוניכי וכסותיכי וסיפוקיכי ומיעל
לותיכי כאורח כל ארעא וצביאת מרת אסתר בתולתא דא
וחזת ליה לאנתו ודן נדוניא דהנעלת ליה מבי אבוהא בין
בכסף בין בדהב בין בתכשיטין במאני דלבושא בשימושי
דירה ובשימושא דערסא הכל קבל עליו צבי חתן דין
במאה זקוקים כסף צרוף וצבי צבי חתן דין והוסיף לה
מן דיליה עוד מאה זקוקים כסף צרוף אחרים כנגדן סך
הכל מאתים זקוקים כסף צרוף וכך אמר צבי חתן דין
אחריות שטר כתובתא דא נדוניא דן ותוספתא דא קבלית
עלי ועל ירתי בתראי להתפרע מכל שפר ארג נכסין וקנינין
דאית לי תחות כל שמיא דקנאי ודעתיד אנא למיקנא נכסין
דאית להון אחריות ודלית להון אחריות כלהון יהון אחראין
וערבאין לפרוע מנהון שטר כתובתא דא נדוניא דן ותוספתא
דא מנאי ואפילו מן גלימא דעל כתפאי בחיי ובתר חיי מן יומא
דנן ולעלם ואחריות שטר כתובתא דא נדוניא דן ותוספתא דא
קבל עליו צבי חתן דין כחומר כל שטרי כתובות ותוספתות
דנהגין בבנת ישראל העשויין כתקון חכמינו זכרונם לברכה דלא
כאסמכתא ודלא כטופסי דשטרי וקנינא מן צבי בן יהודה חרתן
דנן למרת אסתר בת חיים בתולתא דא על כל מה דכתיב
ומפרש לעיל במנא דכשר למיקניא ביה הכל שריר וקים
נאום חתם פ״ה צעיר פב יהו...
נאום ...ש צבור כ...

Akdamot

Yisrael

1.Yi - Yi - Yi - Yis - ra - el, yi - yis - ra - el ve — - o — - rai - ta had - hu.
2.Yi - Yi - Yi - Yis - ra - el, ve - o - rai - ta ve - kud-sha-be rikh Hu had - hu.

Fine

1.ve - o - rai -ta had___ - hu. To - rah o - rah To - rah o - rah
2.vekud sha berikh hu had___ - hu.

Ha - le - lu___ - yah, To - rah o - rah To - rah o - rah

Ha - le - lu___ - yah, Ha - le - lu - yah. Ha - le - lu___ - yah.

D.C. al Fine

Blintzes, Berries, and Kugel

The Talmud says, "When a man comes down to his field and sees a ripe fig, or a perfect cluster of grapes, or a beautiful pomegranate, he ties each with a red thread and says, 'These are *bikkurim,* the new fruits of the festival.'" Shavuot is the summer harvest festival, when the first ripe fruits are blessed and milk and honey are used to symbolize the land of Israel. Dairy dishes such as blintzes and kugel are common as are the honey cakes and pastries also eaten during Rosh Hashana.

The dinner menu included here calls out for guests to share the good food. The blintzes can be made in advance and refrigerated (or frozen). The asparagus can be served at room temperature with a simple vinaigrette instead of the hollandaise. The kugel and the charlotte can also be prepared ahead of time. In all, it's a meal to suit a warm day when you're in the company of friends.

MENU
FORMAL DINNER FOR SIX

◆

Blintzes with Sour Cream

◆

Asparagus with Hollandaise

◆

Poached Snapper with Ravigote Sauce

◆

Kugel

◆

Berry Charlotte

Cheese Blintzes

1 cup flour
1 cup ice water
2 eggs
¼ teaspoon salt
2 tablespoons melted butter
Butter for pan frying

Make a paste of the flour and ice water. Beat the eggs together with the salt. Add to the flour and water. Then add the melted butter. Stir and, if necessary, mix with an electric mixer until the batter is smooth.

Prepare the pan for frying. Drop just enough batter into the hot pan to cover the bottom. Fry on one side until the edges curl away from the bottom of the pan. Toss onto a cloth, fried side up.

Cheese Filling

1 pound pot cheese
1 egg yolk
½ teaspoon salt
1 tablespoon sugar
Butter for pan frying

Mix all the ingredients together thoroughly. Place a heaping tablespoon of the mixture on each of the fried circles. Turn up the bottom side of the circle to begin making an envelope around the filling. Overlap this with the top side of the circle. Fold the sides and tuck in (or just fold the sides in first, following with the top then bottom flaps). Fry on both sides in butter until browned and crispy.

Poached Snapper with Ravigote Sauce

3 pounds snapper or other firm-fleshed fish, cleaned or filleted*
1½ to 2 quarts water
1 cup dry white wine
1 large celery stalk
½ carrot
2 sprigs parsley
1 bay leaf
¼ cup lemon juice
½ teaspoon salt
3 to 5 peppercorns

Wash the fish, inside and out, in cold water. Set aside. Fill a poacher or deep roasting pan with enough water to cover the fish plus one cup. Add the wine. Cut the celery stalk and the carrot into chunks and add to the liquid. Bring to a simmer, then add the parsley, bay leaf, lemon juice, salt, and peppercorns.

When the water is simmering again, add the fish on the poacher's tray or by wrapping the fish in cheesecloth and lowering it into the water. The fish should be covered by at least 1½ inches of water; add more if necessary. Cover, bring to a boil, then simmer for approximately ten minutes, slightly less if the fish is less than one inch thick.

Remove the fish carefully, raising it by the ends of the cheesecloth or with a wide spatula. If the fish is whole, cut into individual portions and bone. Serve with ravigote sauce.

*If using a whole fish, you'll want a 3½ to 4 pound fish.

Ravigote Sauce

1 egg
½ teaspoon salt
4 grinds of freshly ground pepper
1 teaspoon prepared tarragon mustard
1 teaspoon chopped fresh tarragon
1 teaspoon chopped fresh parsley
¼ cup minced onion
3 teaspoons rice wine vinegar
4 to 5 tablespoons olive oil

Hardboil the egg and chop. Combine the salt, pepper, mustard, parsley, tarragon, and onion; mix. Add the vinegar and stir, then add the chopped egg. Whisk in the oil, one tablespoon at a time, adjusting the amount to the desired thickness of the sauce.

Variation:
Add 1½ tablespoons capers, crushed, to the sauce when adding the vinegar.

Asparagus with Hollandaise

2 pounds asparagus

Wash the asparagus and trim the ends. Scrape the top layer off older, larger stalks. Steam the asparagus so that the lower stalk ends are in water, and the tips are not (the steam will cook the tips). Remove the asparagus after 10 minutes; this should be enough time for crisp but cooked greens.

Hollandaise Sauce

½ cup clarified butter
1½ tablespoons lemon juice
3 egg yolks
3 tablespoons boiling water
Pinch of salt

Prepare all your ingredients before you begin cooking. You will need three small saucepans or melting pans and a double boiler.

Warm the clarified butter, being careful not to let it bubble or brown. In a separate saucepan, heat the lemon juice over low heat.

In the double boiler, whisk the egg yolks until they are just beginning to thicken (make sure that the water level in the double boiler is low enough so that the sauce is above the hot water and not in it). Gradually add the hot water, one tablespoon at a time, allowing the yolks to become thick after each addition. Whisk in the warmed lemon juice and remove the yolk mixture from the heat still in the double boiler. Whisk in the warmed butter *gradually* until the sauce is thick. Add the salt and mix.

Serve immediately over the cooked asparagus.

Kugel

1 pound broad egg noodles, broken
2 eggs, separated
2 tablespoons vegetable oil
2 tablespoons sugar
½ teaspoon salt
¼ teaspoon cinnamon
⅛ teaspoon nutmeg
¾ cup golden raisins
½ cup broken walnuts (optional)

Preheat oven to 350°F.

Cook noodles in boiling water until tender; drain, but keep noodles moist. Beat egg yolks, then beat in oil, sugar, and salt. Fold into the noodles. In a separate bowl, combine spices with fruit and nuts; mix well and fold into the noodle mixture. Beat egg whites until stiff but not dry; fold into noodles.

Pour into a well-greased 1½-quart casserole dish. Bake for 45 minutes or until top is browned.

Berry Charlotte

1 pint fresh blueberries
2 pints fresh raspberries
1 pint fresh blackberries
1 loaf of thin-sliced white bread, crusts removed
Approximately ¾ cups sugar
1 teaspoon lemon juice

Rinse the blueberries, raspberries, and blackberries. Let drain. Line a charlotte mold (or other covered pan that slopes gently toward the bottom) with plastic wrap. Make a pattern for the bread slices by cutting out a circle the size of the bottom of the mold and one the size of the top of the mold. Fold the circles in half first and then into thirds. You should now have 6 equal triangles for each circle. Repeat the process to get 6 more smaller triangles. Now trim 6 squares of bread so that they follow the pan's tapering. These squares will be used to line the sides of the pan. Use the triangles to line the bottom of the pan. Do not overlap the bread and try not to leave "holes" in the lining.

Heat the rinsed berries in a noncorrodible pan for 2 minutes. Add the sugar to taste and cook another 5 minutes. Pour the fruit into the lined pan so that it is filled halfway. Make another "bottom" with the remaining smaller bread triangles, then fill the mold to just below the top. Cover with the larger bread triangles.

Stir the juices in the pan used to cook the fruit; add lemon juice and pour the juices over the mold.

Put a plate or cover on top of the mold and weigh it down with at least 4 pounds. Put the mold in a pan or on a plate to catch the juices that will overflow. Refrigerate overnight. Unmold and invert. Serve with whipped cream. Use any remaining berries as garnish.

Tissue Flowers

Materials:
Assorted colors of tissue paper
Pencil
Floral wire or colored craft wire
Floral tape
Scissors

These tissue-paper flowers may be as simple or as detailed as you wish. Tissue flowers are fun and easy to make by both children and adults alike. The individual blossoms themselves may be composed of just a few petals for a dogwood-type of blossom, or layered to resemble a rose in full bloom.

You may choose to make a flower that is composed of dark and light shades of one color or you may use 2 or 3 different colors for a variegated effect. Once you get started, you'll find that experimenting with different effects is fun, and that your results can be very professional. Refer to the photograph as a guide to some of the possibilities.

Getting Started
First, cut out individual flower petals. The tissue paper can be layered to cut 5 pieces at a time, and thus, save cutting time. We find that a petal size of 2″ x 4″ is a good starting size. Only cut out a couple of dozen petals at first so that you can adjust the size later, if you want larger or smaller petals. Remember that tissue paper colors run when wet, so be sure that you have a dry work area.

Curling the Petals
Take one petal and, starting with its point, *loosely* roll half of the petal around the pencil. Slide the pencil out from inside the tissue roll, crinkling the tissue as you remove the pencil (illus. 6A).

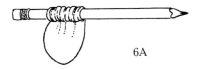

6A

If the pencil is very difficult to remove, you have rolled the tissue too tightly. If the pencil slides out with no resistance at all, you've rolled the tissue too loosely. The resulting petal should have a curled edge and a smooth edge.

Roll additional petals and experiment with the angle of the pencil as you do so: If you hold the pencil at a slight angle on the petal—instead of strictly at a right angle—it will make the curl vary from your first one. Also, try different ways of cutting the petal shapes until you achieve the type that appeals to you.

Assembling the Petals
Bend a piece of floral wire in half and curl the cut ends to resemble the stamen of a flower. This curled part will be seen as you look inside of the paper blossom. Then, think of the way a rose blossom is formed. The inner petals are smaller and tightly

curled. As the blossom matures, the petals unfold wider and have less curl to them. This is how you want to build your petals into the wire.

Lay a petal on the wire and "twist" its flat edge onto the wire. Don't release the petal, since it won't stay on by itself. Place another flower petal on the opposite side of the wire and twist it onto the stem, overlapping the opposite tissue petal. Continue to build up the blossom by adding petals on the wire, twisting each one slightly to connect it to the base. When you have approximately 8 or 9 petals, you are ready to attach the floral tape.

Taping the Blossom
Still holding the blossom with one hand, carefully, but *tightly,* wrap the base of the tissue blossom with floral tape. The tape is very soft and flexible. Stretch it slightly as you wrap the entire stem. Tear, or cut the tape, and wrap the end.

Finishing Comments
These tissue-paper flowers hold their brilliant colors for a long time. They are appropriate for an entire centerpiece or a single-bud vase. In addition, you could make a single blossom for each place setting at a Shavuot dinner.

Photo and Video Tips for the Holidays

As holiday preparations begin, the photographer in the family should begin thinking about how best to capture the spirit of the celebration. Many times the pictures fall short of the memories of the day. The tips below on indoor photography and videotaping will help, but so will a second reading of the instruction manual that came with the camera. For more specific information, refer to the Time-Life series on photography (for single-lens reflex cameras) or to *The Home Video Handbook* (Video-Info Publications, P.O. Box 2685, Santa Fe, NM 87501) or *Home Video Production* (McGraw-Hill Books, 1221 Avenue of the Americas, New York, NY 10020).

Photo Tips

Prepare for the photograph beforehand; look for good background and the best light. Try moving around the subject for a better vantage point and experiment with composition: perspectives from above, below, and to the side rather than straight on.

Try to avoid backlighting—when the sun or other source of light is behind the subject, lighting the background but not the subject. If you can't avoid it, compensate by adding a light to the subject or by opening the aperture $1\frac{1}{2}$ stops beyond what the camera says is correct.

To prevent red-eye in flash pictures, increase the distance between the flash and the camera lens. Although most cameras have flash attachments right on the body, brackets that hold the flash farther away are available and are relatively inexpensive.

For added warmth in a flash picture, use lit room lights to soften the glare. Set the shutter speed to $1/8$, $1/15$, or $1/30$ instead of to the flash synch speed, which is usually $1/60$ or $1/90$. If you don't have a *very* steady hand, invest in a tripod for these indoor shots.

Take two or three shots of the same photograph for those extra-special moments, especially if there is more than one person in the picture.

Video Tips

Prepare for your videotaping. Remember to bring spare batteries, even an AC adapter and an extension cord, for these unexpected emergencies.

Even with the most simple cameras you can plan your shots by making a storyboard, an outline of the video "story." Block off twelve boxes on an $8\frac{1}{2}''$ x $11''$ sheet of paper (three horizontal and two vertical lines should do it) and pencil in what you'd like to see on the finished tape. You may even want to prepare a title card.

Vary your shots; use wide angles and cuts to close-ups as well as zooms.

To make sunlight that is streaming in the windows consistent with the artificial, interior light, place an orange filter over the windows. (The camera perceives sunlight as blue, artificial light as orange.)

Invest in a few optional accessories. Replace standard room bulbs with small quartz photographic lights for a softer effect. A directional mike will pick up sounds at a greater distance, and the quality of the audio is usually better than that of a built-in microphone.

For best lighting results, set up a main light, a fill light, and a back light. The first is usually mounted on the camera straight on or placed just a bit off to the side but still illuminating the subject from the front approximately straight on. The fill light, also called a side light, is positioned about halfway between the camera and the subject, illuminating the subject from this angle. The third light functions to either add depth to the picture or to separate the subject more clearly from the background. For depth, shine the light on the background from behind the subject; for contrast, shine the light from behind the subject onto the subject.

Useful Addresses

General Sources

American Jewish Archives
3101 Clifton Avenue
Cincinnati, OH 45220

American Jewish Historical Society
2 Thornton Road
Waltham, MA 02154

B'nai B'rith
1640 Rhode Island Avenue, NW
Washington, DC 20036

Board of Jewish Education
426 West 58th Street
New York, NY 10019
Jewish Education Hotline

Central Conference of American Rabbis
21 East 40th Street
New York, NY 10016
*Book catalog; A Passover Haggadah
with drawings by Leonard Baskin*

Union of American Hebrew
Congregations
838 Fifth Avenue
New York, NY 10021

Union of Orthodox Jewish
Congregations of America
45 West 36th Street
New York, NY 10018
Kosher products directory

Union of Sephardic Congregations
8 West 70th Street
New York, NY 10023

Book and Magazine Publishers

The Association of Jewish Book
Publishers
838 Fifth Avenue
New York, NY 10021
List of booksellers

Behrman House, Inc.
1261 Broadway
New York, NY 10001
Educational Judaica

Encyclopaedia Judaica
Sadot Agencies Ltd.
14 West Forest Avenue
Englewood, NJ 07631

The Jewish Book Council
National Jewish Welfare Board
15 East 26th Street
New York, NY 10010

Ktav Publishing House
900 Jefferson Street
Hoboken, NJ 07030

Moment Magazine
462 Boylston Street
Boston, MA 02116

Jewish Frontier
15 East 26th Street
Suite 1309
New York, NY 10010

The Jewish Spectator
P.O. Box 2016
Santa Monica, CA 90406

Reconstructionist
Dr. Jacob Staub
Church Road and Greenwood Avenue
Wyncote, PA 19095

Tom Thumb
c/o Gottex Industries
1411 Broadway
New York, NY 10018
Children's magazine

Universe Books
381 Park Avenue South
New York, NY 10016
The Jewish Calendar

Museums

Skirball Museum
Hebrew Union College
3077 University Avenue
Los Angeles, CA 90007

The Spertus Museum of Judaica
618 South Michigan Avenue
Chicago, IL 60605

The Jewish Museum
1109 Fifth Avenue
New York, NY 10028

Judah L. Magnes Memorial Museum
The Jewish Museum of the West
2911 Russell Street
Berkeley, CA 94705

Yeshiva University Museum
185th Street and Amsterdam Avenue
New York, NY 10033

Craftspeople

Daniel Blumberg
333 W. Girard Avenue
Philadelphia, PA 11516
Enamel, precious metals, rare woods

Susan Duhan Felix
1437 Addison Street
Berkeley, CA 94702
Pottery

Edith Fishel
1192 Park Avenue
New York, NY 10028
Pottery

Nancy Golden
14 Clements Road
Newton, MA 02158
Stained glass

Phyllis Kantor
250 East 38th Street
Eugene, OR 97405
Textiles, table linens

Kurt Matzdorf
19 Apple Road
P.O. Box 293
New Paltz, NY 12561
Glass and metal

Rebecca Lynn Wachtel
807 Haines
Champaign, IL 61820
Pottery

Shoshanna Walker
691 Empire Avenue
West Lawrence, NY 11691
or, P.O. Box 7884
Jerusalem 716 307
Israel
Calligraphy, ketubot, megillot

Specialty and Judaica Shops

Brochin's Book and Gift Shop
4831 Minnetonka Boulevard
Minneapolis, MN 55416

Craftwood Lumber Company
1590 Old Deerfield Road
Highland Park, IL 60035
Sukkot kits

Frank's Hebrew Bookstore
1647 Lee Road
Cleveland Heights, OH 44118

Israeli Gifts
575 Seventh Avenue
New York, NY 10018

The Jewish Development Co.
18331-C Irvine Boulevard
Tustin, CA 92680
Gifts, books, gallery

The Jewish Music and Record Shop
147 Essex Street
New York, NY 10002

Kolbo
435 Harvard Street
Brookline, MA 02146
Mail-order gifts, books, etc.

Moriah Art Crafts Inc.
699 Madison Avenue
New York, NY 10021
Antique Judaica

Velvel Pasternak
29 Derby Avenue
Cedarhurst, NY 11516
Sheet-music, cassettes, records, mail-order

Rabbi Piotrkowski's Judaica Center
289 Montgomery Avenue
Bala Cynwyd, PA 19004

Schwartz-Rosenblum
Hebrew Bookstore
2906 West Devon Avenue
Chicago, IL 60659

Emmanuel Weisberg
45 Essex Street
New York, NY 10002
Antique Judaica

Index

PHOTO CREDITS